Pembroke
the premier GUIDE

Published by: Eden Publications Limited 01646 682296
3 Lords Meadow View, Pembroke, Pembrokeshire SA71 4BA

Written by: David Merchant, Matthew Drabble & contributions by local sources

Edited by: Mary Thomas

Photography by: Eden Publications, Miles Cowsill, Gareth Davies, Norman Hughes, Sara Spencer
Pembrokeshire C. C. Tourism & Leisure Services, Mark Deane, Mark Richards, Janet Baxter

Pre-Press Production by: Neil Price Reprographics 01646 650180

ISBN 0 9549562 0 6

FOREWORD BY
BBC BROADCASTER
JAMIE OWEN

Everyone needs a place to think and my place is Pembrokeshire. I grew up here – my bedroom looked out across Milford Haven and for as long as I can remember I've sat and watched the boats sailing past Pembroke Dock – the ferries to Ireland, trawlers from the Bristol Channel, laden tankers from the Middle East – adventures from another world outside my window.

As little boys we learnt to row up and down the River Cleddau from the slip way at Front Street to Lawrenny and back. Our weekends were spent on the beaches of Freshwater and Barafundle. Saturdays and Sundays were always for walks along the coast path – chewing over the past week and thinking about the days to come.

On this ancient coast and its weather beaten shores the cares of the world wash away when you walk over sunken forests that covered Wales millions of years ago.

Pembrokeshire is still the place I return to – the Preseli Mountains where we had picnics, Tenby and the boat to Caldey Island, Broad Haven Beach where we swam in freezing waters – they are the places which anchor my travels everywhere else in the world – the compass to steer by.

Everyone always says you are bound to feel a tie to the place where you were born and brought up but Pembrokeshire exerts a kind of magnetism that makes you yearn for it when you've been away too long. The light is magical – the coastline is mesmeric – the sea hypnotises with its menacing beauty and danger and the people are entrancing.

A. lieu
Swansea 2005

Contents

Croeso

Mae hi yn wastad yn bleser cael croesawu ymwelwyr o rannau eraill o Gymru, a rydym yn hyderus y bydd y llawlyfr hwn o gymorth i chi i wneud y gorau o'ch gwyliau.

Mae'r gyfrol hon yn un o gyfres lwyddiannus Premier Guides a gyhoeddir gan wasg leol Eden Publications, a chaiff ei diweddaru'n gyson er mwyn cadw'r wybodaeth sydd ynddi mor gywir a chyfredol â phosib.

Hwn yw'r llawlyfr mwya cynhwysfawr y gallwch ei brynu ar gyfer y rhan hon o Gymru, gan ddod ynghyd, o fewn cloriau un llyfryn hawdd-ei-ddarllen, fanylion am lu o atyniadau naturiol ac o waith dyn. Mae'r rhain yn amrywio o harddwch cefn gwlad i gestyll o'r Oesoedd Canol, trefi a phentrefi o ddiddordeb hanesyddol arbennig, amgueddfeydd gweithgareddau chwaraeon hamdden, adloniant, bywyd gwyll gwyliau a digwyddiadau, a llawe llawer mwy.

Gallwch gadarnhau manylio agor, prisau mynediad ac ati y uniongyrchol gyda'r atyniadau unigo (mae eu rhifau ffôn yn cael eu rhestr yn y llawlyfr) neu gyda'r Canolfanna Croeso lleol (sydd hefyd yn cael e nodi).

Yn olaf, rydym yn sicr y gwnewcl chi gytuno bod y canllaw hwn yn wertl pob dimau. Felly mwynhewch e ddarllen, a chofiwch gael gwyliau bythgofiadwy a fydd wrth eich bodd.

Bienvenue

C'est toujours pour moi un immense plaisir d'accueillir des visiteurs dont la langue maternelle n'est pas l'anglais et nous espérons sincèrement que ce guide vous permettra de profiter au maximum de vos vacances. Faisant partie d'une série primée de Premier Guides, publiée par la maison d'édition locale Eden Publications, ce volume est mis à jour régulièrement dans le but de garder les informations qui y sont contenues aussi précises et actualisées que possible.

Il s'agit également du guide le plus complet de cette région du Pays de Galles vendu sur le marché, car il donne des renseignements pratiques sur une multitude de choses à faire et d'endroits à visiter, construits soit par la nature soit par la main de l'homme. Ces lieux de visite varient de la beauté du paysage de châteaux, de villes et de villages qui présentent un intérê historique considérable, à des musées, des centres de sports et de loisirs, des lieux de divertissement, des parcs naturels, des festivals et autres spectacles et bien plus encore.

Des renseignements concernant les heures d'ouverture, les tarifs d'entrée et autres renseignements pratiques sont indiqués pour chaque lieu de visite (des numéros de téléphone sont donnés dans toute la brochure) ou dans les Centres d'Information Tourisme (qui sont également listés dans ce fascicule).

Nous sommes convaincus que vous trouverez ce guide indispensable et extrêmement complet pour son prix. Bonne lecture et passez des vacances inoubliables.

Welkom

Het is altijd een eer om bezoekers welkom te heten die een andere taal dan het Engels spreken. We hopen van harte dat deze gids zal bijdragen aan een heerlijke vakantie.

Dit boek maakt deel uit van de serie Premier Guides, bestsellers uitgebracht door Eden Publications. Het wordt regelmatig herzien met als doel de opgenomen informatie zo accuraat en actueel mogelijk te houden.

Het is tevens de meest uitgebreide gids voor dit deel van Wales die er te koop is. Het brengt op eenvoudige wijze en in één band gegevens samen over een hele verzameling natuur- en door de mens gemaakte attracties. Deze variëren van de pracht van het landschap tot middeleeuwse kastelen, steden en dorpjes van groot geschiedkundig belang, musea, sport- en ontspanningsactiviteiten, amusement, natuur, festivals en evenementen, en nog veel meer.

Gegevens betreffende openingstijden, toegangsprijzen, enzovoorts kunnen rechtstreeks bij de individuele attracties (telefoonnummers in deze gids) of bij een plaatselijk Tourist Information Centre (Brits VVV-kantoor) (tevens in deze gids vermeld) worden nagegaan.

Tenslotte vertrouwen we erop dat u het met ons eens zal zijn dat deze gids zijn geld meer dan waard is. Dus veel plezier bij het lezen - en een plezierige en gedenkwaardige vakantie toegewenst.

Willkommen

Es ist uns immer eine große Freude, Besucher, deren Muttersprache nicht Englisch ist, willkommen zu heißen, und wir hoffen sehr, daß dieser Führer dazu beiträgt, das meiste aus Ihren Ferien zu machen.

Dieser Band aus der Reihe der bestverkauften Premier Guides des lokalen Unternehmens Eden Publications wird regelmäßig aktualisiert, um die darin enthaltenen Informationen so genau und so aktuell wie möglich zu halten.

Auch handelt es sich hierbei um wohl den umfassendsten Führer dieser Gegend von Wales, den Sie kaufen können und in welchem die Angaben zu der Unmenge an sowohl landschaftlichen als auch von Menschenhand geschaffenen Sehenswürdigkeiten in einem leicht zu lesendem Buch zusammengefaßt sind. Diese reichen von prächtigen Landschaften bis hin zu mittelalterlichen Schlössern, Städten und Dörfern von großem historischem Interesse, Museen, Sport und Freizeitaktivitäten, Unterhaltung, Tieren auf freier Wildbahn, Festivals und Veranstaltungen und daneben noch vieles mehr.

Genaue Angaben zu Öffnungszeiten, Eintrittsgebühren u.s.w. können direkt mit den einzelnen Attraktionen (Telefonnummern sind im Führer angegeben) oder mit den örtlichen Fremdenverkehrsämtern (die Sie hier ebenfalls aufgelistet finden) verglichen werden.

Wir sind davon überzeugt, daß Sie mit uns einer Meinung sein werden, dieser Führer ist sein Geld wert. Wir wünschen Ihnen viel Spaß beim Lesen - und einen angenehmen und unvergeßlichen Aufenthalt.

PEMBROKESHIRE

Ferry to

Str
H

Pen Brush

Pwll Der

Trefas
St. Nic

Aber Mawr

Abercastle   Grans
Porthgain   Trevine   Mat

A487

Abereiddy   Llanrhian   Square &   Cas
Compass

Croesgoch   Ba
Tretio   Treglemais

Treleddyd-fawr

North Bishop   St. David's   Rhodiad-   Llanhowel   Elandeloy
Head   y-Brenin

Whitesands   B4583   Middle
Point St. John   Whitchurch   Mill   Brawdy   Hav

Bishops   St. Justinian
and Clerks   St. David's

Solva   A487

Ramsey   Pen-y-cwm
Island   Dinas   Newgale
South Bishop   Green   Fawr   Ro

Scar   Simps

Nolton Haven
Nolton   Pe
Lo

Druidston

ST. BRIDE'S   Haroldston West
BAY

Stack   Broad Haven
Rocks   Little Haven

Talbenny   B432
Skomer   St. Bride's   V
Island   Wooltack   PEMBROKESHIRE COAST   C
The Smalls   Point   Martins   NATIONAL PARK
Haven   Marloes   Hasguard

Midland   Sandy Haven   Herbran
Grassholm   Isle
Island   Broad Sound   Gateholm   St. Ishmael's   Milf
Island   Ha

West Dale
Bay   Dale   Milford Ha
Skokholm   Dale   Point
Island   Angle   Rho

Ferry to Rosslare   St. Ann's
Head   Sheep
Island   Freshwate
West

Blucks P

Linney Heac

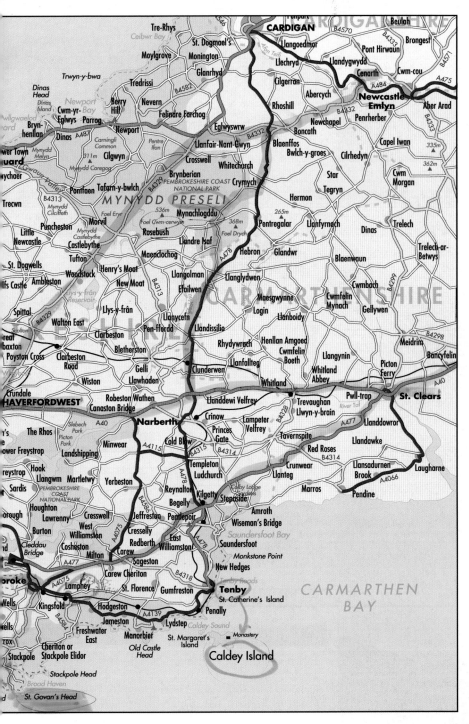

Amroth

European Blue Flag Awards:-
This scheme is for resorts where good beach management is complemented by the quality of the bathing water reaching the highest standard as laid down by current EC legislation. Nine Pembrokeshire beaches currently have European Blue Flag status:
Amroth
Tenby: North, South & Castle
Saundersfoot
Lydstep Haven
Newgale
Whitesands
(St. Davids)
Poppit Sands

Wiseman's Bridge

It is no surprise that many visitors to Pembrokeshire come here first and foremost to enjoy the county's magnificent sandy beaches, now restored to their former glory.

In 2003, no fewer than 30 of Pembrokeshire's beaches qualified for the Tidy Britain's Group Seaside Award. So whether you are a sun worshipper, watersports fanatic, boat owner or you simply love the seaside, Pembrokeshire is an idyllic place to enjoy the great beach holiday.

SOUTH COAST

AMROTH (1)

Amroth is a charming coastal village where time seems to have stood still. The beach is punctuated by a series of groynes that help protect the village from winter storms and rough seas. The Western end marks the start of the renowned 186 mile Pembrokeshire Coastal Path. Parking is good in the village and along the seafront.

WISEMAN'S BRIDGE (2)

The beach's claim to fame is that it was used in 1944 for rehearsals of the D Day landings under the watchful eye of Prime Minister, Sir Winston Churchill himself.

The beach is sandy and it's possible to walk to neighbouring Saundersfoot at low tide. Parking is limited.

COPPET HALL (3)

Coppet Hall is a popular sandy beach which has extensive parking facilities. It also affords access to Saundersfoot village.

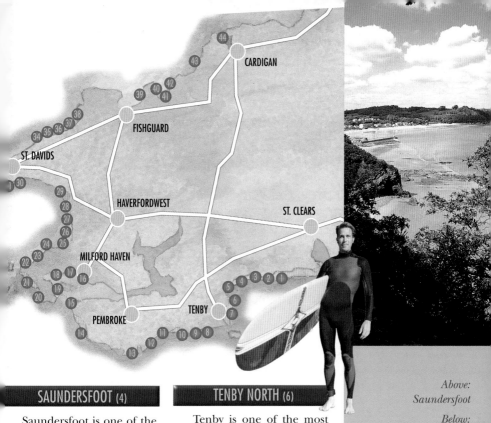

SAUNDERSFOOT (4)

Saundersfoot is one of the area's most popular resorts and it's easy to see why. There is everything for the family including a superb beach and a range of shops, cafés and ice-cream parlours. There is also a picturesque harbour plus extensive parking facilities.

MONKSTONE (5)

Monkstone (Saundersfoot). Unsuitable for families as access is down very steep steps. Those hardy enough to make the journey will find a beautiful stretch of sand but no facilities. Entry to the beach is through Trevayne Farm off the B4316 near New Hedges. There is a small charge for parking.

TENBY NORTH (6)

Tenby is one of the most popular seaside resorts in Wales. A medieval walled town with narrow streets, it stands on a rocky headland, which divides its two main beaches. The award winning North Beach has first class facilities together with a picture postcard harbour and small sandy beach. Because of the town's narrow streets, visitors are advised to park in one of several large car parks outside the town walls all of which are within walking distance of the beaches.

TENBY SOUTH (7)

Tenby's South Beach offers a large expanse of fine sand. A firm favourite with people

Above:
Saundersfoot

Below:
St. Mary's Church,
Tenby

PEMBROKESHIRE'S ULTIMATE BEACH GUIDE

Top: Lydstep Haven
Above: Broad Haven (South)

Skrinkle Haven

holidaying at the nearby Kiln Park Holiday Village. The beach, which is backed by cliffs on which the town stands, offers unlimited views of Caldey Island which is inhabited by monks. Facilities are very good.

LYDSTEP HAVEN (8)

Lydstep Haven is a privately owned beautiful sheltered bay for which there is an admission charge. Characterised at either end by wooded cliffs, Lydstep boasts a slipway to cater for the many boats and pleasure crafts using the bay. One of the area's main features is the Smugglers Cave, which can be explored even at high tide.

SKRINKLE HAVEN (9)

Skrinkle Haven is a absolute gem of a beac' sheltered by tall cliff. However, access is down ver steep steps and a windin path. There is a car park abov the beach but no other facil ties.

MANORBIER (10)

Manorbier is very popula with surfers. Overlooked by medieval castle and the 12t Century church of St. James the beach is the home to stone cromlech known as th King's Quoit. The sandy beac is served by a large car par (charges made during summer) together wit parking areas on the roa above the beach.

Manorbier

FRESHWATER EAST (11)

Freshwater East is a wide, sweeping crescent of sand and shingle backed by dunes and grassy headlands. Popular with boat owners, divers, fishermen and surfers alike, it has a chalet park and caravan site close by. Parking and toilets are available near the beach.

BARAFUNDLE (12)

Barafundle is surely one of Pembrokeshire's most beautiful beaches but is only accessible from the coastal path. Owned by the National Trust, the nearest parking is at Stackpole Quay about half a mile away.

Due to its remote position, the beach itself has no amenities but there is a tea-room at Stackpole Quay.

BROAD HAVEN (SOUTH) (13)

Broad Haven South is a superb sheltered beach popular with sun worshippers. Another of the National Trust owned beaches, it offers excellent parking for both those visiting the beach or for those using it as a gateway to the area's many fine walks.

FRESHWATER WEST (14)

Freshwater West is a haven for surfers. They are drawn to the area by the big Atlantic rollers so it seems only natural that the beach should be the setting for the Welsh National Surfing Championships.

However, it can be dangerous to swimmers because of strong undertows and hazardous quicksands so families with young children should be on their guard.

Freshwater East

Freshwater West

West Dale

Dale

PEMBROKESHIRE'S ULTIMATE BEACH GUIDE

Parking facilities close to the beach are good.

WEST COAST

WEST ANGLE BAY (15)

West Angle Bay is another beautiful location, very popular with visitors and local inhabitants alike. Low tides reveal rock pools, which youngsters can explore. The beach houses the remains of an old limekiln now partly overgrown. There are excellent walks along the cliffs offering spectacular views. Parking and other facilities are good.

GELLISWICK (16)

Gelliswick is the headquarters of the Pembrokeshire Yacht Club and offers an excellent slipway for boats. A large sand and shingle beach, facilities include toilets, free parking and the nearby shops of Milford Haven.

SANDY HAVEN (17)

Sandy Haven beach is sandwiched between the village of Sandy Haven and Herbrandston. Just below Herbrandston lies a sandy beach, which at low tide offers superb views of the estuary. Unsuitable for swimming however, because of unpredictable estuary currents. Parking on both the western and eastern sides of th estuary are limited.

LINDSWAY BAY (18)

Lindsway Bay again is no suitable for bathing, bu because of its position to th Milford Haven waterway, i makes an ideal place fo walking, bird watching and collecting shellfish. Envelope by cliffs and large rocks, it als offers good views of St. Ann' Head from both the beach and the cliff top. South of th bay is Great Castle Head, the site of an Iron Age Fort. The beach is devoid of amenitie and parking is a quarter of a mile away.

DALE (19)

If it's watersports you're after this is the place to be. Dale is home to yachting, windsurfing and a watersports centre. It is also attractive to the sub-aqua fraternity because of its wreck sites. Facilities in the attractive village overlooking the sea are good and there is a large car park opposite the shingle beach.

WEST DALE (20)

West Dale is a stunning, secluded cove, but its sand and shingle beach can be dangerous to swimmers because of undertows and unpredictable currents and hidden rocks. Access is via

Marloes Sands

13

Newgate

2003

The Seaside Award is a UK award scheme encompassing both resort and rural beaches. Its primary functions are to help raise standards of cleanliness, hygiene, safety and environmental management at beaches. The scheme is administered by the Tidy Britain Group. In 2003, it granted a Seaside Award to the following beaches in the County:
Abereiddy
Amroth
Barafundle
Broad Haven (south coast)
Broad Haven (west coast)

(cont. opposite)

road or footpath through Dale but parking is restricted and there are no amenities.

MARLOES (21)

Marloes sands is a magnificent beach, characterised by outcrops of rocks and a large crescent of golden sand at low tide. At its western end is Grassholm - a small island accessible at low tide, which was inhabited from prehistoric to medieval times and which still bears the remains of 5th century huts. Another feature are the Three Chimneys - horizontal beds of rock, more than 400 million years old. The National Trust has a car park half a mile from the beach but the nearest facilities are about a mile away in the village of Marloes.

MARTINS HAVEN (22)

Martins Haven is a small north-facing cove with a pebble beach. Boat trips operate from here to the Skomer Nature Reserve. Facilities include toilets and parking.

MUSSELWICK (23)

Musslewick Sands is a fine sandy beach that is only exposed at low tide. Access is difficult and visitors need to be aware that the tide could cut them off. There are no amenities and parking at the start of the long footpath to the beach is limited.

ST. BRIDES HAVEN (24)

St. Bride's Haven is a sheltered cove with a beach of shingle, pebbles and rock pools, enhanced at low tide by sand. Interesting features near the beach include an early Christian Cemetery with stone lined graves and the remains of an old limekiln. There is limited parking near the church.

LITTLE HAVEN (25)

Little Haven is a small attractive sandy cove with a slipway for small boats, including the local inshore rescue boat. There is a pay and display car park close to the beach and facilities are numerous with pubs offering food and drink together with shops.

BROAD HAVEN (WEST) (26)

Broad Haven (West) is a large, magnificent expanse of sand, which runs the entire length of Broad Haven Village. It is a favourite with bathers and watersport enthusiasts, and also has a great deal to interest geologists with an abundance of different rock formations. The village offers good facilities and a choice of car parks.

DRUIDSTON HAVEN (27)

Druidston Haven, whilst being a long sandy beach, is

Musselwick

Broad Haven (west)

Caerfai Bay

not suitable for bathers because of strong currents. Enclosed on three sides by steep cliffs, access to the beach is by two footpaths. However, there is only limited parking on the roadside and there are no amenities.

NOLTON HAVEN (28)

Nolton Haven is a beach of sand and shingle with cliffs on either side. A Red flag flying warns of danger to swimmers. There is a National Trust car park above the beach.

NEWGALE SANDS (29)

Newgale Sands is another broad expanse of sand exposed to the Atlantic gales, which acts as a magnet to surfers and other watersport enthusiasts. During summer lifeguards designate areas for swimmers and patrol this excellent beach. There are a small number of facilities and parking areas are good.

NORTH COAST

CAERBWDI BAY (30)

Caerbwdi Bay is a small sheltered beach of rock and pebble with sand visible at low tide. Close to St. Davids, it is reached along a half mile footpath leading from the A487 Solva to St. Davids Road where there is limited parking. Although popular with walkers, the beach has no facilities.

CAERFAI BAY (31)

Caerfai Bay is the nearest beach to St. Davids and is popular with bathers, although at high tide the beach is covered leaving only rocks and boulders. A feature of the bay is the unusual purple sandstone along the cliffs, which was used to build St. Davids Cathedral. Parking is available above the beach but there are no facilities.

PEMBROKESHIRE'S ULTIMATE BEACH GUIDE

WHITESANDS (32)

Whitesands, or to give it its Welsh name Traeth Mawr, is consistently rated one of Wales very best seaside resorts, as any visitor will tell you. A large sandy beach in a magnificent setting, Whitesands is well known for its views, glorious sunsets and crystal clear water. It is understandably popular, with safe swimming and surfing areas designated by the lifeguards who patrol here during the summer months. If you can drag yourself away from the beach, there are some stunning walks with memorable views over the St. Davids Peninsula and Ramsey Island. Facilities at the beach are good and include a large car park. As an added bonus, St. Davids, Britain's smallest city is close by with its many attractions and ancient cathedral.

PORTHMELGAN (33)

Porthmelgan is a sandy and secluded beach close to Whitesands. Access is along the coastal path from St. Davids or the car park at Whitesands.

ABEREIDDY BAY (34)

A few miles along the coast towards Fishguard will bring you to Abereiddy Bay which is vastly different to other beaches in the county in that it is covered in black sand - the result of waves constantly pounding the slate cliffs on either side. Tiny fossil graptolites can be found in pieces of shale, which have geological importance and should not be removed. Nearby is the Blue Lagoon, a deep flooded slate quarry, which serves as a reminder that the area was quarried until 1904 when the slate was shipped all round Britain. A large car park overlooks the beach but bathers should take care when going into the water because of undercurrents.

TRAETH LLYFN (35)

Half a mile away from Abereiddy is Traeth Llyfn, a beautiful sandy beach whose only access is down steep steps. The beach is enclosed by cliffs and can be dangerous for swimming, especially in rough seas because of strong undertows. There is also the possibility of getting cut off by the incoming tide. There are no amenities although there is a small clifftop car park within walking distance.

TREFIN (36)

Trefin is not suitable for bathing because of rocks and an unstable cliff, but there are excellent walks and views along the coast in both

Top: Trefin
Above: Pwllgwaelod
Below: Porth Melgan
Opposite: Whitesands

directions. Above the beach where parking is very limited, there are the remains of an old mill.

ABERCASTLE (37)

Abercastle is an attractive sheltered harbour much favoured by fishermen, boat enthusiasts and walkers. Picturesque cottages overlook the shingle beach, which has a small car park. Above the beach to the right lies Carreg Samson - a 4,500 year-old burial chamber.

ABERMAWR (38)

Abermawr is a large sheltered beach covered in pebbles, which is rarely visited by lots of people. Access is along a short path from the road where parking is limited, and although there are no amenities the beach is well worth visiting. Like other beaches in Pembrokeshire, low tide reveals the remains of a drowned forest.

PWLLGWAELOD (39)

Pwllgwaelod near Dinas Head is a small, attractive sandy beach with views of Fishguard Bay and its harbour. It offers good cliff walking, a nature trail and the beach at Cwm-Yr-Eglwys.

CWM-YR-EGLWYS (40)

Cwm-Yr-Eglwys is a petite, eye-catching cove popular with families. Overlooking the picturesque shingle and pebble beach are the remains of the 12th Century church of St. Brynach, which was destroyed during a fierce storm in 1859. The storm also wrecked over 100 ships. Access is along a narrow country lane off the main road between Fishguard and Cardigan but it's well worth a visit. There is limited parking in a private car park.

NEWPORT PARROG (41)

The historic town of Newport stands near the mouth of the River Nevern where there are two beaches - one on each side of the estuary. The Parrog is on the Southern side, and although this is the more sheltered beach unpredictable currents make bathing dangerous. However, the area is rich in prehistoric sites, including Pentre Ifan burial chamber.

NEWPORT SANDS (42)

By far the more popular of Newport's two beaches, this vast expanse of sand on the northern side of the Nevern estuary is backed by dunes and a golf course. A favourite spot for beach games, and all manner of watersports, visitors should be careful of the dangerous currents around the mouth of the river. There is a large car park above the beach and limited parking on the sand.

CEIBWR BAY (43)

Ceibwr Bay is an ideal base for coastal walks as the area boasts the highest cliffs in Pembrokeshire. The spectacular coastal scenery includes the Witches Cauldron - a cave, blowhole and natural arch - together with incredible folding of the cliff rock strata. Another attraction is the sight of Atlantic grey seals swimming offshore or basking on the rocks. Access to Ceibwr Bay is along a very narrow road from the village of Moylegrove with limited roadside parking above the bay.

POPPIT SANDS (44)

Situated at the mouth of the Teifi estuary, Poppit Sands is a very large expanse of sand, which marks the northern border of Pembrokeshire and the northern end of the Pembrokeshire Coastal Path. The proximity of the beach to the town of Cardigan has made it a very popular venue for visitors, but bathers should beware of dangerous currents and heed the warning signs and lifeguard flags. The beach is backed by sand dunes and mudflats, both of which are sensitive, fragile environments important to wildlife, so should be avoided. Facilities close to the beach are good and include a large car park.

Top: Poppit Sands
Above: Abercastle
Below: Ceibwr Bay

Cwm-yr-Eglwys

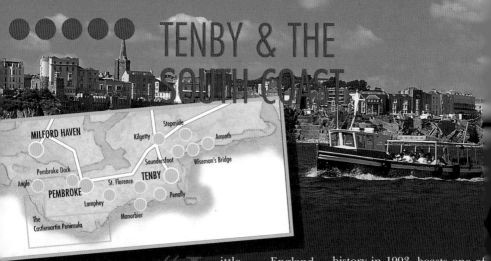

Tenby Harbour

"Little England beyond Wales," is the affectionate term by which South Pembrokeshire is known. The description owes its origin to the Normans who effectively created a linguistic and cultural divide between the north and south of the county when they arrived in Pembrokeshire in 1093.

Today, this divide still exists. South Pembrokeshire is much more English than it is Welsh, while in North Pembrokeshire the reverse is true. However, to visitors the difference is purely academic, and, if anything, adds to the variety of this unspoilt corner of West Wales.

There are four main holiday centres in South Pembrokeshire - Tenby, Saundersfoot, Pembroke and Narberth. Tenby and its near neighbour Saundersfoot are among Britain's favourite seaside resorts, while the ancient town of Pembroke, which celebrated 900 years of history in 1993, boasts one of Britain's best preserved medieval castles. Narberth too is an historic town with a Norman castle.

All four centres are close to the countless visitor attractions and places of interest, and each provides an ideal base for exploring the glorious South Pembrokeshire coastline and countryside.

TENBY

Distances: Fishguard 36 miles; Haverfordwest 19; Milford Haven 19; Narberth 10; Pembroke 10; St. Davids 35; Saundersfoot 3; Carmarthen 27, and London 247.

Little has changed in Tenby since wealthy Victorians provided the finance to develop the town into one of Britain's most attractive holiday resorts.

The Victorians came here for the good of their health, but it was the birth of the coming of the railway in 1866 which saw a ground swell of visitors.

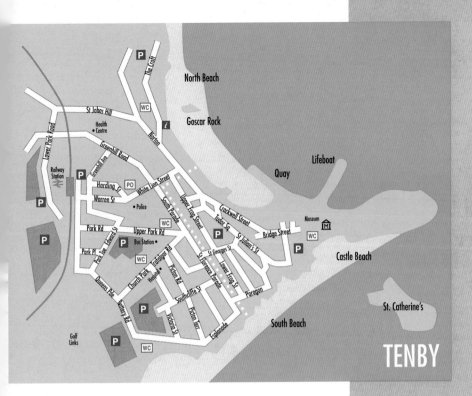

Were those early visitors to return today, they would no doubt be surprised to discover that Tenby is almost as they had left it and has seemingly escaped what many would regard as the "plague" of modern development.

Much of the 13th century wall, which surrounds Tenby is still intact, and the narrow streets, freshly recobbled to imitate a bygone age are still packed tight with shops and eating-places.

Although the bathing machines have long gone, the beaches have still retained their appeal. Both the North Beach and South Beach are a Mecca for holidaymakers. South beach has a bouncy castle and beach trampolines to keep the youngsters amused for hours, and there is a variety of events throughout the season, ranging from beach volleyball to kite surfing.

The picturesque harbour too is unchanged except for the boats. In Victorian time Tenby's link with the sea was dominated by the boats of a once thriving fishing industry as opposed to the leisure craft, which now shuttle visitors to Caldey Island, home to a Reformed Order of Cistercian Monks.

Tenby also offers a great deal away from the beach, here are some of the resort's most popular attractions.

TENBY

Tenby is regarded as one of the jewels in the crown of Pembrokeshire. A haven for holiday-makers since the 18th century, its easy to see why it's so popular. Bordered by two magnificent beaches, the town has retained its character and offers a variety of quality accommodation and good food, whatever your budget.

Tudor Merchant's House, Quay Hill

TENBY'S CAFE CULTURE

Tudor Square in Tenby is an exciting place for al fresco dining. The restaurants and pubs offer patrons outdoor seating during July and August whilst eating dishes from speciality menus and listening to a varied programme of entertainment. The Square is a continental dining experience not to be missed!

Tenby Mural

Described as a panorama of Tenby's history, this magnificent mural by local artist Eric Bradforth is a highly decorative and informative work of art gracing Tenby's refurbished Market Hall. The mural, which measures 32 ft by 8 ft reveals a wealth of detail about Tenby's past, including the building of the town walls together with the arrival of the Pembroke and Tenby Railway in July 1863. It also depicts many of the people who made their mark on the town.

A detailed explanation of the paintings historical content is available from the Tenby Museum and Art Gallery.

For further information ring 01834 842809.

Castle Hill

Overlooking Tenby harbour, and with panoramic views across Carmarthen Bay to Worms Head and the Gower Peninsula, Castle Hill is where you will find the Welsh national memorial to Prince Albert, Consort to Queen Victoria, which was inaugurated by Prince Arthur in August 1865.

Another tribute to the Victorians is the replica bandstand, built in 1991 where regular musical performances are given every summer.

Tenby Harbour

Small, picturesque and brightly coloured by the neat painted cottages and spectrum of summer sail; Tenby harbour has a magnetic attraction. To sit on the harbour wall watching fishermen cast their lines and the boats sailing to and from Caldey Island is a pleasurable way of whiling away the time. Alternatively, you can explore the lifeboat station, passing Laston House on the way where in the 19th century, Sir William Paxton played his part in helping to put Tenby on the map as a fashionable resort.

Tudor Merchant's House

Tenby's 15th century Tudor Merchant's House is the oldest furnished residence

in the town. Standing on Quay Hill, between the harbour and Tudor Square, its authentic furniture and fittings recreate the atmosphere of the period and illustrate the manner in which a successful Tudor merchant and his family would have lived. Three of the interior walls bear the remains of early Frescoes. Owned and managed by the National Trust, the house is open between April and October every day except Wednesday.

For further information ring 01834 842279 or 01558 822800.

Tenby Lifeboat Station

Tenby is fortunate to have two lifeboats - the RFA Sir Galahad and the smaller inshore rescue boat, the Georgina Stanley Taylor. The Sir Galahad is housed in the main boathouse close to Castle Hill, which was established in 1852. There, visitors can see a detailed record of many of the 1800-plus lives saved by the station's boats and crews in over 140 years of voluntary service.

The station is open to the public from mid-May to the end of September between 10.30am and 5.00pm, Monday to Friday and 2.00pm to 5.00pm on Sundays. Additionally, during August it opens 7.00pm to 9.00pm, Monday to Friday, free admission. The new lifeboat station opens September 2005 for further information go to website: www.tenbyrnli.co.uk

Tenby's North Beach

Top: Five Arches
Above: Caldey

Caldey Island

A visit to Caldey Island is like stepping onto a different world. The monastery and ancient churches combine with the sea air and quiet, beautiful surroundings to create Caldey's unique atmosphere of timelessness and peace.

Caldey is more than just an island with a monastery. You can enjoy a snack at the Tea Gardens, try the unique perfumes made on the the island, visit the Chocolate Factory and Weaver's Shop, choose an unusual gift or send a postcard franked with the island's special stamp. You can watch a video about the life of the monks and explore the Old Priory and the island's simple and inspiring churches. A walk up to the Lighthouse offers spectacular panoramic views of the Pembrokeshire coast and beyond. You can also follow the waymaked cliff and woodland paths, or simply relax on the lovely sandy beach at Priory Bay.

Caldey is just a 20 minute boat trip from Tenby. Boats run every 20 to 30 minutes between 10am and 5pm, from Easter to the end of October. Sailings are Monday to Saturday from May to

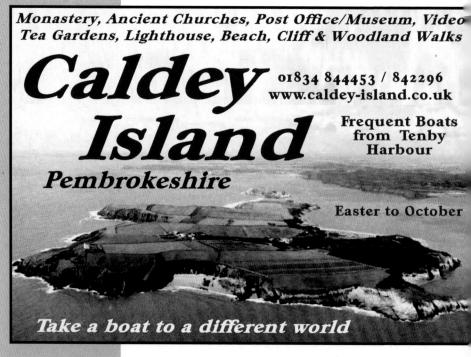

eptember, Monday to Friday in April
nd October. The island is closed on
undays. Tickets can be obtained from
he Caldey Island kiosk at the top of
Tenby harbour.

*For more details Tel: 01834 844453
website: www.caldey-island.co.uk.*

A full range of Caldey products can
also be found at the Caldey Island
Shop, Quay Hill, Tenby.

De Valance Pavilion

This impressive 500-seater hall in
Upper Frog Street in the heart of
Tenby hosts a great variety of entertain-
ment throughout the year.

*For details of the 2005 programme of
entertainment and events, ring 01834
842730.*

Fecci & Sons

Once upon a time (or Easter 1935
to be exact), Mr. Fecci and his four
sons opened the doors of their fish
restaurant in the pretty seaside town of
Tenby for the first time and took the
grand total of ten shillings and
sixpence ... 52½p in today's money! To
celebrate this grand and lucrative
opening, they cracked open a bottle of
French champagne which no doubt
cost somewhat more than the days

NEW YEAR CELEBRATIONS

It's not only in the summer months that Tenby attracts the visitors. Wintertime too has its followers, with Christmas and the New Year being a favourite time with revellers. New Year's Eve in particular is celebrated in style with thousands of people congregating in the town's Tudor Square to welcome in the New Year.
In nearby Saundersfoot, they hold a New Year's Day swim where hundreds of hardy entrants take a plunge in the sea - all for charity.

Right:
Tenby's South Beach

Below:
Tenby Harbour

takings but nevertheless signalled the beginning of a long, prosperous and very popular business venture.

It would appear that the secret of their continued success and popularity lies in sticking to their two rules ... quality assured Pembrokeshire Potatoes 'rumbled' on the premises and only cut into chips as required and the purchase of all fish fresh from the docks at nearby Milford Haven.

They have since won numerous awards in national competitions for the Best Fish & Chip Shop. Pay them a visit in Lower Frog Street, Tenby and judge for yourself.
Tel: 01834 842484.

Silent World Aquarium

Housed in an attractive 19th century chapel close to North Beach, Silent World is home to a fascinating and intriguing collection of over 200 marine species, a large collection of reptiles, exotic creepy crawlies and leaf cutting ant colony. As well as

fish and other creatures from the local shores, seas, rivers streams and lakes of Pembrokeshire, you'll also be able to see more exotic fish such as seahorses, amphibians and invertebrates and dramatic species of snakes and lizards from around the world. Daily handling and feeding sessions are held.

For more information ring 01834 844498.

Tenby Arts Festival Saturday 17-24 September

Many visitors and local residents have discovered over the years that one of the best times to be in Tenby, is during its Arts Festival in late September.

The Festival has established a fine tradition of offering a full and varied programme, to suit a wide range of tastes and interests. Traditionally it opens with a weekend of family fun, launched by a grand parade of entertainers through the streets of the town. These two

The Fountains

**Takeaway -
Hot & Cold
Food**
Breakfasts
• Rolls &
Sandwiches
• Teas • Coffees
Ice Cream Kiosk
Snacks available
all day

Cafe and Beach Shop
South Beach, Tenby

Beach Shop
Buckets & Spades,
beach balls,
inflatables, kites,
beach games,
hats,
sunglasses, beach-
wear, suncream and
much, much more ...

Open early 'til late. We can fully provide for your day on the beach!
Large car park right next to beach

days also feature a sand sculpture competition for all the family, kite-flying and other colourful events around the beach and harbour.

The main eight- day festival provides a feast of music, dance, film, poetry, art, drama and talks in a diverse programme, featuring international names as well as favourite local artists.

Programmes will be available in the Summer from information centres, libraries and other outlets throughout Pembrokeshire. Further details can be obtained by ringing 01834 843839 or visiting the website at: www.tenbyartsfest.co.uk

Tenby Leisure Centre

Facilities include swimming pool and children' learner pool; multi-purpos sports hall and fitness room.

For more information rin, 01834 843575. See Activit Section.

Tenby Museum & Gallery

Founded in 1878, Tenb Museum and Art Gallery i one of Tenby's main indoo attractions, with the reputa tion of being one of the bes local museums in the country Situated on a spectacular site in part of the medieval castle overlooking Castle Beach and Caldey Island, the museum is a

Caldey Island

easant place for visitors of all ges to explore.

The galleries show the eology and archaeology of embrokeshire, its natural history, its bygones and the hanging aspects of Tenby's evelopment up to the present day. Minor exhibits nclude the last invasion of the British mainland by the French in 1797, and the Pembroke and Tenby Railway. The Local History gallery features special temporary exhibitions on the history of Tenby and South Pembrokeshire.

The art gallery concentrates on artists with close local associations, and works by others which portray Tenby and its locality. There is a significant collection of the work of the early 19th century topographical artist Charles Norris.

Augustus John was born in Tenby, and his sister Gwen, now becoming the more highly regarded, was brought up here. There is a permanent exhibition of their works, and from time to time, more extensive displays which include works loaned by other collections. Another Tenby born artist represented is Nina Hamnett, an English Modern. Many others, such as Graham Sutherland, are featured in the annual summer exhibition, which runs from Easter to October.

Tenby Museum

St Catherine's Island, off Tenby

Ritec Valley Quad Bikes

The Museum and Art Gallery is open throughout the year. Full access for disabled visitors. Admission charges and concessions apply. *For more information & opening times ring 01834 842809.*

PENALLY

Nestling just west of Tenby is the pretty hillside village of Penally, which overlooks Tenby's golf course and South Beach. Penally is a well-kept village complete with post office, shops and pubs together with a good choice of accommodation including a first class hotel, camping and caravan sites.

A feature of the village the 13th century church of S Nicholas, which houses memorial to the victims of th Tenby lifeboat who drowne when it capsized in 183 Penally's proximity to Tenb Lydstep, Manorbier, Fresh water East and Pembroke makes it an ideal holiday spot

Ritec Valley Quad Bikes, Penally

Ritec Valley Quad Bike offers the ultimate in Qua Bike entertainment whateve the weather! Trail Rider (Minimum age 16) will not b

...sappointed with over 10KM of routes encompassing some of the finest man-made and natural terrain.

Sessions need to be booked in advance. Trail riding is only open from February Half Term until October Half-Term. Arrive and Drive is open all year round and minimum age is 6. Arrive and Drive is ideal for youngsters or families wishing to ride together.

All kit is supplied and includes Helmets, Waterproofs, Goggles and Wellingtons.

New for 2005 is a PC Network gaming centre. Play the best games against your friends!

For further information ring, 01834 843390. Check our website out at: www.ritec-valley.co.uk, or e-mail: info@ritec-valley.co.uk.

Heatherton Country Sports Park, St Florence, Tenby

Situated in acres of picturesque parkland near the village of St. Florence, Heatherton offers a great day out for families of all ages - with a bonus! There is no entry fee. You only pay for the activities you participate in. Economies can also be made through family packages and group deals.

Horseriding at Heatherton Country Sports Park, St. Florence

Penally from the Golf Course

Attractions include: Maize Maze, Pirates of Caribbean Adventure Golf, Coarse fishing, Paintball games, Archery, Clay pigeon shooting, Pistol shooting, Karting Track, Bumper Boats, Baseball, 18-hole pitch and putt course and Horse riding centre.

For further information, ring 01646 651025.

ST. FLORENCE

Once a medieval harbour standing on an inlet to the sea, St. Florence is a picturesque village of great charm and pretty cottages and boasts being a past winner of the national "Wales in Bloom" competition. Here you wi discover one of the area's la surviving curious roun chimneys, which are ofte described as Flemish in styl Also of interest is the 13t century parish church featuring a Norman tower.

SAUNDERSFOOT

This bustling village about three miles from Tenby lying at the foot of a pic turesque wooded valley. Wit its attractive harbour and extensive sandy beaches, it ha established itself as a popula centre for sailing, fishing

atersports and traditional seaside olidays.

Originally a small fishing village nd home to two ship-yards by the 800's, Saundersfoot was suddenly aught up in the excitement of the lack gold rush when high quality nthracite was discovered locally. uch was the demand for this coal hat in 1829 the harbour was built, onnected by rail to six mines. The ailway ran along what is now The Strand, and the coal was exported worldwide.

It was not until the Second World War that coal shipments ceased, but oy this time another flourishing ndustry was putting the village on he map - tourism. The rest as they say is history.

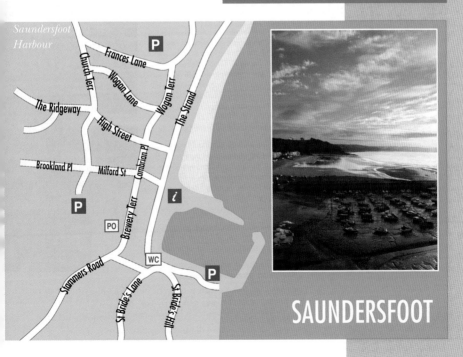

SAUNDERSFOOT

Amroth

AMROTH

The small coastal village of Amroth sits on the Pembrokeshire and Carmarthenshire border, just seven miles from Tenby and four miles from Saundersfoot. It is a wild and beautifully unspoilt location. In summer the wonderful expanse of gently shelving sand, exposed at low tide, makes it a favourite beach for families and anglers alike.

The village, spread along the narrow seafront, lacks the frills of bigger resorts but has an undeniable charm together with plenty of good facilities - including restaurants, pubs, gift shops, caravan parks and holiday home Attractions close by includ Colby Woodland Garden which is owned by th National Trust, and Pendin Sands - a resort made famou in the 1920's by speed king Si Malcolm Campbell.

Llanteglos Estate, Llanteg, Nr. Amroth

Llanteglos Estate offer secluded self-catering holi days. Llanteglos House wa built as a large country residence over 130 years ago Situated in the leafy seclusior

---

Llanteglos Estate

SECLUDED
SELF-CATERING
Holidays

Llanteg House was built as a large country residence over 130 years ago. Situated in the leafy seclusion of the original orchard and gardens, the Lodges enjoy a relaxing peacefulness, complemented by spacious lawns and children's play area for our guests to enjoy.
Pets Welcome.

Llanteg,
Near Amroth,
Pembrokeshire
SA67 8PU

Woodland Lodges (WTB 4 Star) There are eight Woodland Lodges built in a staggered terrace arrangement. They are designed to take full advantage of their elevated south-facing aspect, with the bathroom and bedrooms downstairs and lounge kitchen/dining area upstairs. The lodges sleep up to six in double and twin rooms plus sofabed. This affords the opportunity to step through patio doors on to a large balcony with a commanding vista of National Parkland forestry and glimpses of the sea of Carmarthen Bay. These Lodges are particularly suitable for early and late holidays.

Orchard Lodges The twenty four Orchard Lodges, built in groups of four, were architecturally designed to blend with their surroundings. Each lodge can sleep up to six in a double 'gallery' bed plus twin and bunk bedded rooms. There is an open plan living area and kitchen; bathroom and patio area outside.

Garden Lodge (WTB 3 Star) Newly converted guest rooms, all en-suite are now available for those who prefer bed & breakfast (all rooms non-smoking).

The Wanderers Rest Popular on-site pub and music venue, open to non-residents. Real ales and pub meals.

The Wanderer's Rest Inn

For more information or a copy of our brochure contact us on
(01834) 831677 or 831739
Fax: (01834) 831279 e-mail: llanteglosestate@supanet.com
www.llanteglos-estate.com

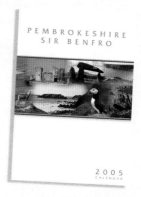

of the original orchard and gardens, the Lodges enjoy a relaxing peacefulness, complemented by spacious lawns, tennis court and children's play area for their guests to enjoy.

Tel: 01834 831677 or 831739 for further information.

Above: Parry Thomas driving 'Babs' in which he set a new World Land Speed Record of 171.02 m.p.h. on Pendine Sands, April 1926. The following year he died at the wheel of 'Babs' while attempting to regain the record.

The car was buried in the sand by local villagers with th consent of his family and wa recovered for restoration i March 1969.

WISEMAN'S BRIDGE

This tiny hamlet, bes known for its inn and rock beaches, nestles on the coas road between Saundersfoo and Amroth and a low tide it i possible t walk across the sand to either You car also walk to Saundersfoo through the tunnels that once formed part of the all important railway link between local mines and Saundersfoot harbour.

STEPASIDE

It is hard to believe now but in the 19th century this

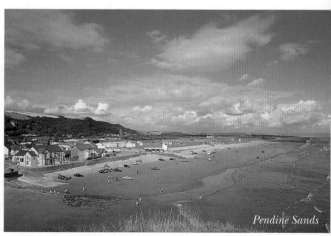

Pendine Sands

quiet little hamlet was a hive of industrial activity after the Pembrokeshire Iron and Coal Company built the Kilgetty ironworks here in 1848. Iron ore, in plentiful supply from seams along the cliffs between Amroth and Saundersfoot, was smelted in the blast furnace using locally produced limestone and coal and the iron transported to Saundersfoot harbour by railway. However, from the outset, the ironworks were beset by major problems, and it ceased operations less than forty years after going into production.

South Pembrokeshire from the east went through Kilgetty village. However, the place remains an important centre for visitors, with its Tourist Information Centre, railway station, supermarket and shops, and it's close to several major attractions. The neighbouring village of Begelly is well known for Folly Farm and is a short distance west of Kilgetty are the villages of Broadmoor and East Williamston, where there are first class caravan parks, a pub and a garage offering cycle hire.

Colby Woodland Garden

Described by the National Trust as one of their most beautiful properties in Pembrokeshire, the garden is part of the Colby Estate, which was established by John Colby, the 19th century mining entrepreneur. The garden is a spectacular blaze of colour from early spring to the end of June. On site is a National Trust shop where refreshments are available, along with gallery, plant sales, toilets and a car park.

For more information ring 01834 811885.

KILGETTY

Before the bypass was built, the main road into

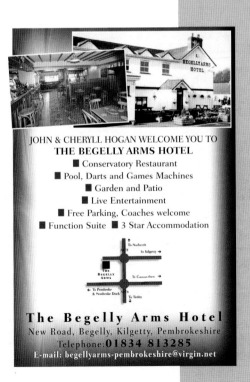

TENBY & THE SOUTH COAST

Kilgetty Tourist Information Centre, Kingsmoor Common, Kilgetty

The Centre is run by The Landsker Borderlands Tourism Association.

Tel: 01834 814161 or visit the website at: *www.visitpembrokeshire.com*

Begelly Park Gardens

Set in 12 acres of natural and landscaped features, including Japanese Garden, one and a half acre lake, woodland walk, spring wildflower meadow and many

Manorbier Castle

pools and fountains.

There is also a lakeside picnic area and tearooms. Dog are welcome on leads.

The Gardens are ope from Easter to Septembe 10.00am - 6.00pm *(phone fo winter openings).*

Tel: 01834 811320

MANORBIER

Manorbier is a smal seaside village midwa between Tenby and Pembroke, and best known fo two striking features - the beach and a well-preserved medieval castle. The castle.

THE DIAL INN

Only a stone's throw from the Bishops Palace, this elegant, interesting and deceptively large village pub has excellent bar food and wine list, plus an imaginative evening menu, freshly prepared and cooked.

Also available are fine wines and cask conditioned ales. The Inn is open for coffee, lunch, dinner and bar meals.

Listed in AA & Which
CAMRA award
Good Food Guides

Families and Children Welcome
Bed & Breakfast
Pool Table and Darts .
Squash Courts at rear
Spacious En-suite accommodation
Non Smoking Areas
Pembroke 2 miles

Lamphey, Pembroke
Telephone: (01646) 672426

*Lamphey
Bishop's Palace*

which enjoys a spectacular location overlooking the bay was the birthplace of Gerald of Wales, a much-respected medieval writer and man of many talents whose two major works are still in print today. But Gerald wasn't the only one to find inspiration in Manorbier. George Bernard Shaw spent several months there and prior to her marriage in 1912 Virginia Woolf was a regular summer visitor.

The Bier House

The Bier House in the centre of the village was built in 1900 to house the parish bier - a funeral hand cart that was used to carry the dead to the burial ground. Now the building has been restored and provides an information point relating to the history of the parish.

LAMPHEY

The village of Lamphey is the site of what is left of the Bishop's Palace, built in the 13th century by the Bishops of St. Davids and now in the care of Cadw who are responsible for Welsh Historic Monuments. The centuries old ruins are an evocative reminder of the great power enjoyed by the medieval bishops of St. Davids. The comfortable palace buildings were set among well-stocked fishponds, plump orchards and an extensive vegetable garden. In its heyday, Lamphey boasted an impressive 144-acre park, a deer herd, windmill, two watermills and a dovecote. The palace's finest architectural features include the great hall built by Bishop Henry de Gower in the 14th century, and the 16th century chapel.

The ruins are open daily from 10.00am - 5.00pm. Admission prices: Adult £2.50, Conc. £2.00, Family ticket £7.00.

For more information ring the Pembrokeshire Tourist Information and Visitor Centre on 01646 622388 or CADW (Welsh Historic Monuments) on 02920 500200.

Pembroke Castle and Millpond

With such a splendid setting overlooking a beautiful unspoilt beach, families love to explore Manorbier Castle and bring a little bit of history to life.

The impressive Great Hall, Chapel and Turrets are dotted with life size figures – see children of the Tudor period and some prisoners in the dungeon.

Look out for Gerald of Wales – the great twelfth century scholar who was born here, and described the Castle as "the pleasantest spot in Wales."

The car park is conveniently situated between the Castle and the beach, so you can enjoy a great family day out at the Castle **and** one of Pembrokeshire's loveliest beaches.

Opening times:
Daily from Easter to
30 September
9.30am to 5.30pm
Admission:
£3.50 adults
£1.50 children
£2.50 senior citizens
Dogs admitted only on a lead. Picnics welcomed.
Excellent local transport:-
Bus no. 349
Tenby-Haverfordwest stops at the gate.
Train station ¾ mile away
Tel: 01834 871394
www.manorbiercastle.co.uk

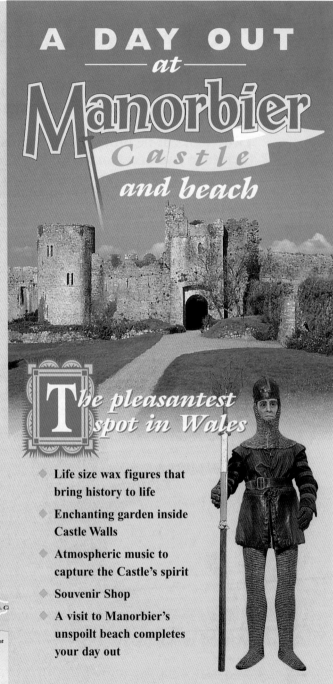

A DAY OUT
at
Manorbier
Castle
and beach

The pleasantest spot in Wales

◆ **Life size wax figures that bring history to life**

◆ **Enchanting garden inside Castle Walls**

◆ **Atmospheric music to capture the Castle's spirit**

◆ **Souvenir Shop**

◆ **A visit to Manorbier's unspoilt beach completes your day out**

PEMBROKE

Distance: Fishguard 26 miles; Haverfordwest 10; Milford Haven 5; Narberth 15; St. Davids 26; Tenby 12; Carmarthen 32 and London 252.

Pembroke is a small but charming walled town with a genteel atmosphere and a 900 year-old history and much to commend it to visitors.

Like many other Welsh towns, Pembroke grew up around its medieval castle. This magnificent structure, the birthplace of Henry Vll enjoys a spectacular location offering breathtaking views from the top of its famous round keep. The castle is in a very good state of repair having undergone an extensive restoration programme that started as far back as 1928.

Throughout the year, the castle is the venue for many important events, several of which are traditions rooted firmly in the town's medieval past. The castle also plays host to such attractions including Shakespearean productions, medieval banquets, military tattoos and displays by the Sealed Knot Society.

The Norman Conquest saw Pembroke develop into the main base from which the invaders increased their stranglehold on West Wales. The town became a major market centre, with regular fairs. Now every October, this tradition is still remembered when the town celebrates the Pembroke Fair which attracts visitors from far and wide.

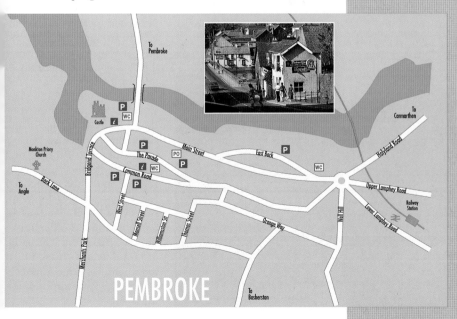

The vast majority of Pembroke's shops, banks, restaurants and many of its most impressive Georgian houses are to be found along Main Street - a pleasant thoroughfare with facades ranging from Tudor to modern. Here visitors will discover an interesting mix of retail outlets, including those run by the Pembrokeshire Coast National Park together with the National Trust and Pembroke Visitor Centre.

Another of the town's attractions is Mill Pond, formed by one of two tidal creeks, which helped give Pembroke Castle its excellent defensive position. It's a popular beauty spot with locals and visitors alike because of the wildlife it attracts. Swans, herons, cormorants and if you are lucky enough even otters can be seen along this peaceful stretch of water.

As visitors explore Pembroke, they will see evidence of the town's ancient and extensive walls, which are a throwback to the 13th century, when the townsfolk demanded that stone walls be built to protect their cottages from raiders. It took 30 years to complete the task, the remains of which can still be seen today.

Since the Norman Conquest 900 years ago, Pembroke's fortunes have been mixed. Under Norman rule it established itself as an important trading port and hit a peak between the 17th and 19th centuries exporting goods around Europe only to fall into decline with the coming of the railway. The situation was compounded by the gradual silting up of the shallow river entrance.

By the end of the Second World War the town was relatively poor and overlooked for large-scale development. But every cloud has a silver lining and in 1977, Pembroke was designated an Outstanding Conservation Area, which today attracts large numbers of visitors from around the world.

Above:
Pembroke Castle

Below:
Mill Pond, Pembroke

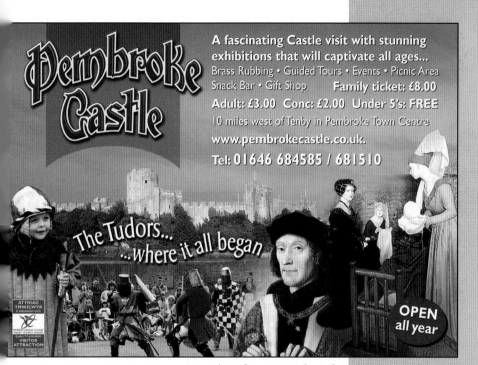

Pembroke Festival 2005

Although still very much in its infancy, the Pembroke Festival has firmly established itself in the Pembrokeshire cultural calendar.

Held over ten days in early September, the Festival aims to showcase the best local musical and artistic talent, while at the same time bringing top professional performers to the historic walled town.

It is a mixture which has proven highly popular during the Festival's first two years, and with everything from storytelling and water-sports to guided walks, cookery demonstrations, puppetry, street theatre, art and craft exhibitions and live music of very kind, there's always something for everyone.

The main events take place on a specially erected marquee in the grounds of Pembroke Castle, but there's always plenty more going on around town throughout the week. So if you're heading down West in September, make a date to visit this year's Pembroke Festival.

Pembroke Visitor Centre

Built in 1993 to coincide with the town's 900th birthday celebrations, this is an integral part of Pembroke's superb new Tourist Information Centre. Displays and exhibits tell the story of Pembroke, and there is a choice of books, maps and souvenirs on sale.

For further information, ring 01646 622388.

Pembroke Castle

Pembroke Castle is one of the best-preserved medieval castles in Wales. Open to visitors all year round it is an

TENBY & THE SOUTH COAST

Pembroke main street

intriguing place to explore. The wide walls are honey-combed with a seemingly endless system of rooms, passageways and spiralling flights of narrow stone steps; interpretative displays and information panels give a fascinating insight into the castle's origins and long history. One of the most impressive features is the distinctive round keep, which was built soon after 1200. It is 75 feet high and the views from the top in all directions are nothing less than magnificent.

From this lofty position it is very easy to understand why the Normans were well aware that the site was ideal for fortification - a low rocky peninsula between two tidal creeks offering superb natural defences. They quickly established a wooden fortress, and in 1200 began work on the castle itself.

Harri Tudor (Henry VII) was born in Pembroke Castle on 28th January 1457 of an Anglesey family. In 1485 he returned from exile in France landing at Millbay on the Milford Haven waterway. From there he marched a growing army of largely untrained volunteers across country to Bosworth Field in Leicestershire to confront Richard III. Against the odds, Henry'

heavily outnumbered forces defeated Richard and Henry became King of England. So ended the Wars of the Roses and began the Tudor dynasty.

For further information, ring 01646 681510 or 684585.

Henry's Gift & Coffee Shop

A visit to Henry's Gift and Coffee Shop is a must for all discerning shoppers. Situated in a listed building in the shadow of Pembroke Castle, Henry's is an Aladdin's cave for those seeking quality gifts and local memorabilia for friends and family, seven days a week.

The gift shop stocks a large selection of presents for all occasions, including glassware, china, linen, jewellery, prints by local artists, Ty Beanie Babies and delightful floral arrangements together with greetings cards, gift vouchers, candles, cushions and lots, lots more.

Henry's now has an extensive China and Glassware department stocking such brands as Royal Worcester, Aynsley, Portmeirion, Poole Pottery, Wedgewood, Conwy pottery: as well as being Pembrokeshire's only stockists of Spode and Royal Crown Derby.

If shopping isn't your forte - why not take time out to enjoy a coffee and eat delicious cakes while reading one of the wide selection of daily newspapers.

Snacks and light lunches are also served in the fully licensed coffee shop, where there is local fare like homemade soups, daily specials, scones, Welsh cakes and Bara Brith to tempt even the most delicate palate. Please book on 01646 622293 to avoid disappointment.

Opened ten years ago, Henry's Gift and Coffee Shop is a popular destination for holidaymakers and locals alike, and is the kind of place you can spend hours browsing around or just relaxing.

Details of our opening hours, menus and current stock can all be viewed at www.henrysgifts.co.uk

Top: Castle Hill cottages

Above: The Barbican Gate, Pembroke Castle

47

PEMBROKE DOCK

Pembroke Dock

Pembroke and Pembroke Dock are alike in only one respect: both have experienced fluctuating fortunes. There the similarity ends, because as a place of any significance Pembroke Dock has a very short history.

In the early 19th century it was nothing more than a small coastal village known as Paterchurch. But when in 1814 the lease expired on the Royal Naval Dockyard in Milford Haven, the Admiralty decided to move its shipbuilding operation across the water and further inland from the mouth of the estuary - and Paterchurch was designated the ideal site. Hence began an amazing transformation, which saw naval architects lay out the distinctive grid pattern of wide streets so characteristic of present-day Pembroke Dock. The prosperous new town grew up around the thriving dockyard, and many fine ships were built here. These included HMS Tartar, the first steam man-of-war; HMS Conflict, the first propeller-driven warship and several royal yachts.

When the dockyard closed in 1926 it had produced more than 260 ships, and the town's

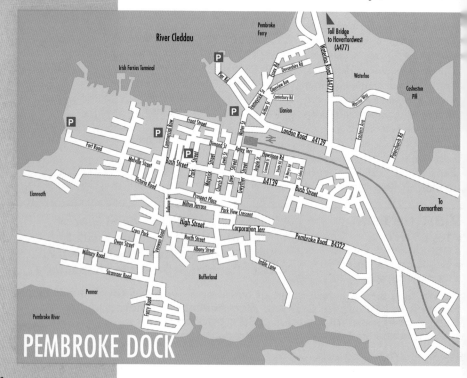

PEMBROKE DOCK

PEMBROKE DOCK
LONDON ROAD
TELEPHONE: **01646 687962**
OPEN 7.30am - 11pm SEVEN DAYS A WEEK

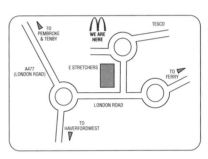

HAVERFORDWEST
CARADOG WELL ROAD, MERLINS BRIDGE
TELEPHONE: **01437 769513**
OPEN 7.30am - 11pm SEVEN DAYS A WEEK

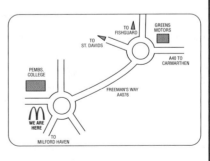

The old Llanion Barracks Armoury

population exceeded 3000. But it was not long before ships were replaced by a totally different kind of boat. In 1930 a major part of the dockyard site was transferred from the Admiralty to the Air Ministry, and in the following year the Royal Air Force established a seaplane base, operated by Southampton flying boats of 210 Squadron. 1938 saw the arrival of the squadron's first Sunderland flying boat - the aircraft with which Pembroke Dock is most associated. During the Second World War the Sunderlands gave sterling service and eventually stayed on here until 1957. Even today the aeroplanes are far from forgotten, and on occasions their spirit are revived in startling fashion. In March 1993, for example, during one of the lowest tides of the century, three men discovered the remains of a rear gun turret and fairing - part of Sunderland flying boat of 20 Squadron that crashed in the Haven waterway during training exercise in March 1954.

Today, Pembroke Dock i better known as a ferry por with excellent boating and watersport facilities. The Cleddau toll bridge, at 15(feet high, gives spectacula views over the waterway in both directions. The Cleddau Bridge is, in fact, a very signifi cant landmark because once you have crossed it to the waterway's northern shore you have left South Pemb- rokeshire behind.

The Gun Tower Museum

The Gun Tower formed part of the fortifications of the Milford Haven waterway. The tower's specific role was to

The Gun Tower

Sunset over the Cleddau Bridge

help defend and protect the Royal Naval dockyard, though in the event the only threat came from air raids in the Second World War - long after the dockyard had closed.

Built in 1851 to repel "unwelcome guests", the imposing dressed stone tower now welcomes visitors with open arms. Visitors are offered an intriguing experience of the life lived by Queen Victoria's soldiers and marines - who awaited, in these cramped quarters, the French invasion which never came.

Three floors of colourful models, pictures and full scale displays include life sized soldiers and many authentic relics. These build up an exciting picture of Pembroke-shire's military heritage.

A splendid panoramic model shows us the town's Royal Dockyard. Here 250 warships were built, along with five elegant royal yachts. A whole room is devoted to the RAF. During World War II, Pembroke Dock was the world's largest operational flying boat base.

Important features include an original working roof cannon and the basement magazine, where 20,000 lbs of gunpowder were stored, plus an educational video. Among new exhibits are a majestic 12-foot wingspan model Sunderland flying boat, and a display of authentic World War II aircrew uniforms and equipment.

The museum is open seven days a week from 10am to 4pm and charges a small entry fee. ***For further information ring 01646 622246.***

THE CASTLEMARTIN PENINSULA

The Castlemartin Peninsula, which is also known as the Angle Peninsula, typifies the unique appeal of South Pembrokeshire in that it has many special features of interest to many different groups.

The magnificent scenery which unfolds along the coast path, and the profusion of wild flowers and butterflies to be found here captivates sightseers, walkers, photographers, artists and naturalists.

Birdwatchers flock here for the colonies of guillemots, razorbills, kittiwakes, choughs and other species that nest along the cliffs and rock formations.

To geologists, the peninsula presents some outstanding examples of fissures, sea caves, blowholes, natural arches and stacks - the result of continual sea erosion of the carboniferous limestone cliffs.

Above: Looking towards Grenala Point

Below: St. Govan's Chapel

Anthropologists have been excited by the discovery of bones and implements in caves which 20,000 years ago gave shelter to the region's earliest-known human inhabitants.

Historians are enchanted by such mysteries as tiny St Govan's Chapel and by the remains of Iron Age forts and other ancient sites.

And for visitors who are here simply to enjoy a holiday there are attractions such as the Bosherston lily ponds and the superb beaches of Barafundle, Broad Haven, Freshwater West and West Angle Bay to savour.

The peninsula is also well known for its 6000-acre Ministry of Defence tank range. This means that a large section of coastline is inaccessible - one of the very few places where the Pembrokeshire Coastal Path is diverted inland - but there is some compensation to visitors, in that on certain days a spectator area enables you to watch the tanks in action as they fire live ammunition at a variety of still and moving targets.

Much of the southern half of the peninsula, including the tank range, was once part of the Stackpole Estate. This embraced more than 13,000 acres and was one of the most substantial land holdings in Wales. Until 1688 the estate was owned by the Lort family of Stackpole, but in that year it

changed hands when Eliza-
beth Lort married Alexander
Campbell of the Cawdor
Estate in Scotland. It was the
enterprising Campbells who
created the Bosherston lakes
and lily ponds. They also
planted a great variety of trees
and introduced many unusual
and innovative ideas to the
estate, including the building
of a stone icehouse - an 18th-
century refrigerator in which
dairy produce was stored. In
1976 the National Trust
acquired 2000 acres of the
estate and is now responsible
for its management. Sadly,
though, the mansion that
stood on the estate - Stackpole
Court - was demolished in the
1960's.

FRESHWATER EAST

From the small coastal
village of Freshwater East,
visitors are ideally placed to
explore the stunning coastline
of the Castlemartin Peninsula.
Stackpole Quay, Barafundle
Bay, the Bosherston lily ponds
and Broad Haven beach are all
within very easy reach along
the coast path, while only
Barafundle is inaccessible
by road.

Freshwater East is also a
popular resort in its own right.
The Trewent Park holiday
complex provides self-catering
accommodation close to the
beach, and there are shops, a
touring caravan park and
other facilities.

STACKPOLE

Stackpole has its name in
Norse origins, and the village
as it stands today is in a
different place from its
original medieval site, having
been moved by the Campbells
in 1735 to accommodate
growth of the Stackpole
Estate. The centre of the old
village is about half a mile to
the southwest, marked by the
remains of a preaching cross.

Close to the present village
are interesting areas of
woodland - Castle Dock,
Cheriton Bottom, Caroline
Grove and Lodge Park - which
were planted as part of the
estate 200 years ago. There are
species here from all over the
world, many of them brought
in from London's Kew
Gardens. The woods are
managed by the National
Trust, who have created
several miles of pathways for
horses and walkers.

STACKPOLE QUAY

The National Trust owns
and manages Stackpole Quay,
which it acquired in 1976 as
part of the 2000 acres of
Stackpole Estate. This acquisi-
tion also included the stretch
of coastline between here and
Broad Haven, under the
Enterprise Neptune initiative -
a scheme launched by the
Trust in 1965 to save and
protect Britain's precious and
threatened coastline.

Stackpole Quay

Stackpole Quay was originally a private quay built for the estate, so that coal could be imported and limestone shipped out from the quarry. It is claimed that this is Britain's smallest harbour, however pleasure boats are now the only craft that use the stone jetty.

There are good parking facilities here, as well as toilets and a new National Trust information centre and cafe. This car park is as close as you can get by road to nearby Barafundle beach, which is accessible via the coast path.

Stackpole Quay is also notable for its geological features. Fossils of old shells and corals can be seen in the rocks, and just to the east of the quay is a change in the cliff landscape, where the grey carboniferous limestone gives way to deposits of old red sandstone.

STACKPOLE QUARRY

As part of its management of the Stackpole Estate, the National Trust has utilised the natural geological features of the old quarry near Stackpole Quay to create an area in which visitors - including those with special needs - can enjoy countryside recreation. Around the top of the quarry is a circular path giving spectacular vistas of the surrounding landscape and coastline. Down below, on the quarry floor, are sheltered picnic and barbecue areas and an archery bay. In addition, the cleared rock faces present a challenge to experienced climbers and abseilers.

Everyone can use the quarry's facilities, but group or event organisers should first contact the warden. Close to the quarry is the main car park for Stackpole Quay, along with National Trust holiday cottages, carefully converted from old buildings.

For more information about holiday lets ring 0870 4584411 www.nationaltrust.org.uk and for details of the quarry facilities, ring the Trust's Stackpole office on 01646 661359.

BOSHERSTON

For such a small village, Bosherston certainly enjoys its share of fame due to its proximity to several major tourist attractions in South Pembrokeshire. These include the delightful Bosherston lily ponds - part of the Stackpole lakes - and Broad Haven beach. On days when the M.O.D tank range is not in use and the access roads are open, Bosherston is also the gateway to remarkable St. Govan's Chapel and some of the best limestone cliff scenery in Europe, with coastal features such as St. Govan's Head, Huntsman's Leap, Stack Rocks and the Green Bridge of Wales.

The village is also home to the 14th-century St. Michael's Church which has an unusual cross of the same period standing in the churchyard, and much older still is a huge boulder, originating from Scotland, which was deposited at Bosherston by a moving glacier during the last Ice Age.

Bosherston also has ample parking (with alternative parking above Broad Haven beach) and a pub, tearooms and toilets. When the tank range access road is open, there is also plenty of free parking at St. Govan's.

To find out in advance when the range access roads will be open, ask at any Tourist or National Park Information Centre, or ring Merrion Camp direct on 01646 662287 or Bosherston Café on 01646 661216. Details are also published in the local press.

BOSHERSTON LILY PONDS & BROAD HAVEN BEACH

When the Campbells of Stackpole created the lakes and lily ponds to enhance their estate in the late 18th and early 19th centuries, they were unwittingly setting the scene for an attraction that now brings thousands of annual visitors to the small village of Bosherston.

Covering more than 80 acres, the lakes and lily ponds are the largest area of fresh water in the Pembrokeshire Coast National Park, and are part of the Stackpole National Nature Reserve. They are usually at their very best around June, when the lilies are in full bloom, but even in winter they provide easy and fascinating walks. They also offer good coarse fishing and are well stocked with roach, pike, tench and eels. Fishing permits are available from the cafe in the village.

There are in fact three lakes, artificially created by the deliberate flooding of narrow limestone valleys. The lily ponds occupy only the western lake, which is fed by underwater springs. Grey herons are regular visitors, and the total lakes area attracts a great variety of birds and wildlife, including coots, moorhens, mallard, teal, swans, cormorants, kingfishers, buzzards, and many smaller winged visitors, such as blue damselflies and emperor dragonflies. Over 20 species of duck alone have been recorded here.

ST. GOVAN'S CHAPEL

Remarkable St. Govan's Chapel is one of the wonders of Pembrokeshire. A tiny building hidden in a fissure in the cliff near St. Govan's car park, the restored chapel nestles at the bottom of a flight of narrow stone steps. It is said

Bosherston Lily Ponds

that if you count the steps on the way down and then count them on the way back up, the numbers won't tally! This is only one of the mysteries and legends attached to the chapel.

Though it occupies the site of a 5th-century hermit's cell, the age of the chapel itself is not known for sure; expert estimates put it at no older than 11th-century. St. Govan is reputedly buried here beneath the altar, and it is also said that Sir Gawaine, one of King Arthur's knights, lived here in isolation. Yet another legend tells of the holy well's miraculous healing powers.

St. Govan's Chapel is close to St. Govan's Head - the most southerly point in Pembrokeshire, and well worth seeing for its dramatic cliff scenery. Both are accessible via the road that runs through Bosherston village.

HUNTSMAN'S LEAP

According to legend, a horseman fleeing from pursuers miraculously leaped across this gaping chasm in the cliffs west of St. Govan's Chapel. On looking back he was so horrified by the prospect of what might have happened that the shock killed him anyway!

CASTLEMARTIN

In the small village of Castlemartin is a circular stone cattle pound, built in the 18th century, which now serves as traffic roundabout. There is another connection here with cattle in that the land, rich and well drained because of the carboniferous limestone is some of the most fertile in Wales and was at one time renowned for its high cereal yield and breed of Castlemartin Welsh Black cattle.

Close to the village is the tank range spectator area which when open gives free admission to cars and coaches Just east of Castlemartin is Merrion Camp itself, where two tanks stand on display at the main gates. When the range is not in use there is access to Stack Rocks car park. From here it is only a short walk to the spectacular Green Bridge of Wales - a natural limestone arch - and the two vertical rock stacks that give rise to the name Stack Rocks. In early summer these rocks are a cacophony of calling seabirds as thousands of breeding guillemots and razorbills cling to every ledge, nook and cranny.

FLIMSTON CHAPEL

This medieval chapel, used as a barn until it was restored, is now open to visitors and stands beside a deserted farm on the Castlemartin tank range. It is accessible along the road to Stack Rocks car park (which is open only when

Huntsman's Leap

Angle Bay

the range is not in use). It is dedicated to St. Martin, and in the churchyard, where boulders deposited by glaciers have been used as gravestones, stands the stone Ermigate Cross.

STACK ROCKS

Also known as the Elegug Stacks, these two tall pinnacles of rock standing close to the cliffs at Stack Rocks car park are literally bursting with life in early summer, when they are home to thousands of nesting guillemots, razorbills, kittiwakes, fulmars and gulls. The name Elegug is South Pembrokeshire dialect and a corruption of heligog, which is the Welsh word for guillemot.

GREEN BRIDGE OF WALES

Standing just 150 yards or so from Stack Rocks car park, the Green Bridge of Wales is an excellent example of a natural limestone arch. It was formed by the joining of two caves, each created by erosion of the rock through constant bombardment by the sea, and eventually the roof of the arch will collapse and leave a pinnacle of rock - a stack - standing in the sea. This is the same process that created Stack Rocks. The Green Bridge of Wales is easy to see and photograph in full profile

- with complete safety - thanks to the wooden viewing platform constructed specially for the purpose by the National Park Authority.

ANGLE

The village of Angle, sandwiched between the popular sandy beach of West Angle Bay and the pleasure craft which moor in East Angle Bay, is at the entrance to the Milford Haven waterway, and has a long seafaring tradition. It also has a lifeboat, housed in an impressive modern station, and a number of interesting features. Among its historic buildings are a medieval fortified residence (known as the Tower House), the scant remains of a castle, a dovecote, and 15th-century Angle Hall. Also surviving are long, narrow fields which are rare examples of the strip system of farming which the Normans introduced in the late Middle Ages.

Angle and the surrounding area is superb walking country. In addition to the delights to be discovered on the coast path, there is much to see along the Haven waterway, where giant supertankers and small sailing dinghies share an unlikely co-existence in one of the world's best natural deep-water harbours.

The Green Bridge of Wales

Readers who wish to explore the area are recommended to follow Tour 3 in the Car Tours section.

TENBY & THE SOUTH COAST

TENBY

Blueberry's Restaurant
A bustling, bright, continental style restaurant

D. Fecci & Sons
Award winning licensed gourmet fish and chip
restaurant and take-away with extensive menu   ***see inside front cover***

Fecci & Sons De-Valence Lounge Cafe
Ice cream parlour and coffee shop with over
100 mouth-watering titles to choose from   ***see page no. 25***

Five Arches Tavern and Restaurant
A highly recommended venue with a variety of
homemade dishes on the menu

Fountains Cafe
A friendly cafe providing eat-in or takeaway food,
conveniently situated on South Beach.   ***see page no. 27***

The Pam Pam Restaurant
A popular restaurant with a large and varied menu

SAUNDERSFOOT

The Royal Oak
Enjoy restaurant fayre, fine wines and a great range of
beers in a friendly atmosphere. Sunday lunches and fresh
local fish a speciality   ***see page no. 33***

BEGELLY

The Begelly Arms Hotel
Conservatory Restaurant Carvery/á la Carte
light meals, teas, bar and garden   ***see page no. 37***

MANORBIER

Chives Tea Room
Morning coffee, lunches and afternoon teas
from Easter to September   ***see page no. 38***

LYDSTEP

The Lydstep Tavern
Good food and fine ale in a traditional
Country Inn   ***see page no. 38***

LAMPHEY

The Dial Inn
Excellent bar food and wine, plus an
imaginative evening menu   ***see page no. 39***

PEMBROKE

Henry's Gift & Coffee Shop
Fully licensed, with delicious home cooked light lunches
and afternoon teas, open until 7.00pm June to Sept. ***see page no. 46***

The Corn Store
Take refreshments in our waterside cafe
with fresh locally sourced produce, open 9am - 5pm ***see page no. 42***

LAWRENNY

Quayside Tearoom
Beautiful homemade cakes, Pembrokeshire clotted cream teas,
freshly baked baguettes, local crab and daily specials all
served in a magnificent waterside setting. ***see page no. 147***

PEMBROKE DOCK

McDonald's Restaurant
Good fast food for the whole family!   ***see page no. 49***

If you wish to be included in our next
"Where to eat" section of this guide
then please telephone us on
01646 682296 for further details.

PEMBROKESHIRE'S PREMIER ATTRACTIONS

The Dinosaur Park Gumfreston, Tenby

Walk with the dinosaurs at The Dinosaur Park

At the Dinosaur Park, Tenby on the mile long **Dinosaur Trail** deep in the woodlands, on the boardwalks over swamps where over 20 life size dinosaurs are waiting to meet you. A few tips…Mother Triceratops roars out if you get too close to baby Tiny Tops and close examination of the Pteranodon eggs brings a screech from Terry. Look out for the hissing raptors devouring a carcass (they might mistake you for lunch!). Roger the T-Rex is always hungry so steer clear of his snapping jaws and tiptoe past Eric the spitting Dilosophaur otherwise you may get wet! This is just a taste of what you'll encounter. If you survive all this, complete the **free quiz** and earn your 'Expert' sticker.

Visit Dino's Den Adventure Playland with a custom built indoor Adventure Playground for tougher and bigger kids alongside a brilliant Soft Play Den with 3 separate areas, and Little Tykes Toys where even the tinys can join in. Heaps of fun for everyone! It's perfect for birthday parties too.

In the Adventure Playground big kids can whoosh down the Giant Astro Slide, whilst toddlers can go on the **Dippy Dinoslide**. Blast away as you wiz round the **Orbiter Car Circuit**, drive your own motorised tractor as a **Dino Keeper on Safari.**

Dance on the water in the battery run Disco Boats. **The Jungle Climb and Jurassic Challenge** will also test your skills. Get your licence on the brilliant **Off-Roaders Circuit** or reach for the sky on the **Superjumper trampolines.**

Little ones will be busy feeding the pets and working the Diggers in **Excavator Alley** or making sandcastles in the sandpit. All the family can compete on the free 18-hole **Volcanic themed Adventure Golf Course.**

A changing programme of Daily Activities in our Theatres

Fossil Hunt - every child guaranteed a fossil.

Puppet Show - lots of participation.

Dinosaur Crafts - make something to take home.

Family Frolics - Monster style "It's a Knockout".

Pat-a-Pet - at Guinea Pig Village.

Treasure Hunt - search for dino clues.

Children's Street Entertainer - lots of clowning around and fooling about!

All activities are supervised so every child can take part.

In the Activity Centre Computersaurus Alley offers screens for all ages and skills - educational games and CD ROMs.

Operate a life - size T-Rex head and make it roar and blink; examine a dinosaur egg nest and fossils and see live hatchlings' in an incubator. Youngsters can even climb into a nesting box and hatch a dino egg.

New activities for **2005** are **Dino Frisbee** - bag a dino with the amazing aerobic rings, get lost in the lanes of the **Labyrinth** and twist and glide on **the Magic Rollers.** When you're ready to eat choose from the **Rib Cage Restaurant** with its dinosaur - themed menu, daily "specials" and toddler size meals or sit on the **Sun Terrace** by the self - service kiosk, or join Dino in his Den at the **Snack Bar** - there's something for all tastes.

Come early for a Monster Day out for the whole family.

Dinosaur Park, Tenby located on the B4318 Sageston to Tenby road.

Fun at Folly Farm

Folly Farm - Wales' Premier Family Attraction

Folly Farm Family Adventure Park is one of Wales' largest family attractions situated in the heart of Pembrokeshire. Heading north from Tenby on the A478 towards Narberth you will find Folly Farm less than a mile from the Kilgetty Roundabout.

Daily entertainment ensures a fun-packed day for the whole family. Special events take place throughout the season, including a variety of magnificent shows in the theatre and the Jolly Barn.

Meet and learn about many exciting species of exotic animals such as meerkats, ostrich, monkeys and zebra at the Zoo. There are even a number of endangered species belonging to the European breeding programme including bongo, Arabian oryx, porcupine, and Brazilian tapir.

See the dairy cows being milked in the parlour and visit the Pets Centre where under supervision you can cuddle rabbit or guinea pig. Enjoy the popular bottle-feeding extravaganza and meet many more of the farms resident animals.

For the exhilaration of the racetrack try the Formula 2 go karts. The karts can accommodate a small child with accompanying adult.

Travel back in time at Folly Farm's old time Fun Fair. Rekindle the spirit and nostalgic atmosphere of yesteryear in the massive under

cover complex. In Europe's largest undercover vintage fair you can take a spin into fantasy on the 1922 Golden Gallopers, see the fair from the air on the chair-o-planes, brave the ghouls in the ghost train, dodge your mates on the bumper cars and ride the caterpillar. There are many more rides to excite and make you dizzy this truly is a unique experience not to be missed. The newest rides include the vintage Eli bridge big wheel and giant helter skelter.

If that's not enough to tire the kids out then pack them off on a voyage of discovery on the pirate ships and other adventure play equipment while you relax and unwind with a refreshment from the Dog and Duck licensed bar.

After all that excitement take advantage of a relaxing countryside walk. Regular tractor and trailer rides will transport you to and from the nature trail that meanders through the scenic Pembrokeshire landscape.

Folly Farm has plenty to offer including restaurants, burger bar, gift shops and much, much more.

At Folly Farm the fun never stops, regardless of the weather, look out for their brochure or call them for more information on 01834 812731. Don't forget to visit the Folly Farm Shop in Tenby high street. If you have internet access why not check out the website at www.folly-farm.co.uk

Feeding Time at Folly Farm

Heatherton

Heatherton Country Sports Park, St. Florence

Heatherton Country Sports Park, near Tenby in Pembrokeshire offers the family a chance to test their skill and speed in a day of action.

Situated in acres of picturesque parkland near the village of St. Florence, Heatherton Country Sports Park offers exactly what it says in the title. It is a great day out for families of all ages, children big and small – with a bonus! There is no entry fee. You only pay for the activities you participate in. Economies can also be made through family packages and group deals.

Have an adventure in a maize maze where fun combines with challenging discovery to give you the time of your life.

Start your journey with some fun mazes, straw mountain, huge sand pit, panning for precious stones or play zone and then venture into the giant Maize Maze. This three dimensional twister will turn you inside out, stir your senses and blow your mind!

Enjoyed by all ages, it's the ultimate 3-D challenge of your life, a great adventure and a taste of the living countryside naturally!

If you are after some fun for the whole family and yo don't mind getting lost, the this is the ideal experienc with over 3 miles of pathway bridges, numerous dead end and various puzzles to sol along the way, but remembe this crop won't last forever! S bring your camera, kid courage and sense o adventure and enjoy your da at one of the finest Maiz Mazes in the world.

Pirates of the Caribbea Adventure Golf set on on acre of land, the 18-hol course comprises of lon; undulating fairways, sanc bunkers, water hazards, cha lenging contours and uniqu par 4 and 5 rated hole combine to create the lates and greatest craze i miniature golf. Scaled dow versions of signature hole from world famous course help to create an exciting anc truly challenging miniature golf course.

This realistic miniature golf course com-bines the stimulating play and unique challenge of a regulation style golf course with the lates themeing from Disney. As you start your game you will be met by our very own talking parrot who will tell you the story of past pirate conquests and will warn you of the dangers that lie ahead. As you continue to make your way around the course be sure to avoid capture and don't get

Heron's Brook

aught on the pirate ship as it comes under cannon fire. To set the scene you will find yourself amongst palm trees, cascading waterfalls and other exotic plants. This is truly an experience not to be missed and can be enjoyed by the whole family.

Coarse Fishing, with two lakes to choose from and both newly stocked with Carp, Tench, Roach and Rudd there will be something to tempt even the most experienced of anglers. For those of you who have never tried this sport before, but have always wanted to or maybe you just forgot to pack your rod, do not worry, as we can provide everything for you; rod, bait, licence and friendly instruction if required. All this is set in picturesque surroundings, allowing for a perfect days fishing.

For the more adventurous members of the family, **Heatherton Paintball Experience** is guaranteed to get the adrenaline pumping and your hair standing on end as you experience armed combat through testing countryside.

You will be given many tough tasks in varying challenging terrain. You could find yourself defending forts and huts, hiding in bunkers and tunnels, or planning an offensive through streams and trenches. If you are up to the challenge you may be able to capture a village, kidnap the president or plant a bomb. This activity is suitable for both groups and individuals. All the latest equipment is provided.

All the old favourites are also still available. There are a wealth of activities to try and as all activities are led by experienced instructors and all equipment is provided, you don't need to be an expert at anything.

To test skill and nerve, there are targets such as **archery, clay pigeon shooting, pistol shooting** and of course **paintball.**

For some friendly family barging, the **Karting Track** and **Bumper Boats** are firm favourites. There are Karts to suit all ages and plenty of rubber on both to ensure no tears are shed.

Baseball buffs can pit their talents against a mechanical pitcher and attempt to hit a home run. If baseball is a little too hectic, try the **18-hole pitch & putt course** which has just been redesigned and expanded.

If you'd prefer to witness some of Pembrokeshire's most picturesque countryside in a more tranquil surrounding **Heatherton Riding Centre** will be ideal for you. Whether you are experienced or a complete beginner there will be a horse or pony suitable for you. You can choose from

PEMBROKESHIRE'S PREMIER ATTRACTION

Heron's Brook

one hour, one and a half hours or half day treks. You will be provided with safety hats, and will be under the expert supervision of our friendly qualified staff. Replace lost energy at our fast food restaurant or you could visit our outdoor barbecue and picnic area to catch a breath between the non-stop action and adventure.

So why wait to enjoy a day to remember for the whole family which is guaranteed to be your wildest day out in Wales. *Tel: 0871 434 1349.*

Heron's Brook

Heron's Brook Anim Park and Golf Course on th outskirts of Narberth suits tastes whether it's animals exciting rides - and what more the weather makes litt difference to the enjoyment.

With over twenty show and events throughout the d: there's more than enough satisfy the hunger of even th most demanding visitor.

If animals bring a smile your face, at Animal Magic yo can meet the friendliest dee donkeys, sheep, pigmy goa

nd pot bellied pigs not forgetting, of course, 200+ ducks and geese roaming freely eager to be hand fed.

This is also the chance to cuddle your favourite pets from fur to feather in our Pat-a-Pet demonstration building.

For budding commandos and those who enjoy action Heron's Brook has an aerial cableway, adventure playground, and battery operated trikes and tractors. An Astroglide mat slide and rat-lesnake alpine ride should also keep young and old alike entertained.

The new Forest of Myths and Legends awaits all young knights and fair maidens who are brave of heart and stout of mind, for within lurks creatures of myth and fairytale legends.

Ardent golfers are not forgotten. The park's nine-hole pitch and putt course has drivers averaging 50 yards, ideal for children and beginner. For the more experienced and adventurous there is the 18 hole Approach Golf Course which has drives averaging 100 yards. Mature trees, green hugging bunkers and a landscaped lake make it a very challenging Par 3 to Par 4 course.

An added bonus is that golfing equipment is free although balls are 50 pence each. So beware of the rough!

The courses are open every day from March until October from 10 am until dusk, and weekends only throughout the winter.

However, if it's a lazy day you want, the extensive landscaped gardens at Heron's Brook could be just what you are looking for. Relax or picnic in our terraced gardens, while the children discover Merlin's Maze before taking in a leisurely game of crazy golf or bowls.

If a flutter on the horses is more your style, why not try something different - like sheep racing. Be the owner of a woolly jumper for this hilarious steeplechase (main season only).

At Heron's Brook, our friendly staff ensure that learning is fun in our daily demonstrations and activities, and with over 10,000 sq ft under cover it's a great day out that even adverse weather can't spoil.

We have facilities for the disabled with mother and baby changing rooms. Car parking is free and dogs are allowed if kept on a lead.

For more information ring 01834 860723 or 860023 or visit our web site at www.herons-brook.co.uk or e-mail us on info@herons-brook.co.uk

Oakwood's Bounce

Oakwood
Wales' Largest Theme Park

Oakwood Leisure Park is one of the UK's top ten theme parks and Wales' top paid-for tourist attraction with 400,000 visitors each year. Boasting over 40 rides and attractions you can be sure of a great day out for the whole family! Oakwood opens this year on March 24th with special events throughout the year so keep checking our website for the latest information on what's happening in 2005.

Oakwood's sizzling Summer spectacular After Dark runs from the 29th July until the 30th August. Join in the party atmosphere when the park remains open until 10pm every evening! Experience live family entertainment at its best with our indoor shows at 6.30pm, 7.30pm and 8.30pm where our professional cast will this year thrill you with four decades of hits. Enjoy a drink at Oakwood's tropical island Bali H'ai and experience the thrill of the rides by night before gathering by the outdoor stage to celebrate the end of a great day out. "Disco Inferno" this year's outdoor show will get you in the party mood and set the scene for an explosive finale with our fabulous fireworks display. And don't forget for the daytime entry price you can enjoy the park all day and all night or come after 5.30pm a discounted rate in time f the After Dark celebrations.

For Halloween Oakwoo will again play host to ghos and ghouls for Eerie Evenin from the 26th until the 30 October. With cauldrons o the boil you can pre-book spooky supper in ou Cemetery Wood Restauran enjoy a fantastically spooky liv show in our Haunted Taver and ride our rides in the dar But watch out when darkne falls...you never know wha might go bump in the night!

Amongst the world clas white-knuckle entertainment Hydro – where you can expec to get wet! Europe's talles steepest and fastest wate coaster, Hydro opened in 200 amid good company. Megafobia is Oakwood' award-winning wooden rolle coaster, voted best in the worl for four consecutive years an best wooden roller coaster o the last Millennium Described as the closes sensation to free flight imagin able, Vertigo is a 50m high sky coaster that soars at speeds o up to 110kph in 1.5 seconds And The Bounce is the UK's only 160ft Shot 'n Drop Tower coaster which shoots riders into the air at speeds of 70 kph and 4 G-Force in less than two seconds.

These internationally-acclaimed rides are set amidst some great all-time family

COASTER COUNTRY
OAKWOOD
PEMBROKESHIRE

ll up on FUN at OAKWOOD

Oakwood

favourites – Plane Crazy, The Pirate Ship, Treetops Coaster, Brer Rabbit's Burrow, The Waterfall, The Bobsleigh, The Skyleap, Snake River Falls, Crazy Golf, Pedaloes on the Boating Lake and much, much more. Family fun for everyone!

For smaller kids there's plenty of fun to be had in KidzWorld – a special world created just for children. In KidzWorld your child can lead an expedition into the under-cover adventure playworld The Lost Kingdom where a host of physical challenges await them. WhizzKidz can experiment with more than 30 hands-on science exhibits in the indoor discovery world Techniquest. In The Wacky Factory, they'll have a ball! Equipped with thousands of soft balls, banana blasters, air fountains and levi-tation tables all propelled by compressed air, The Wacky Factory is an interactive play zone where kids can go wild! And for the little ones there's Playtown, where kids can ride the Clown Coaster, pilot their own jet plane or cause chaos on the roads in their own Trucks.

Oakwood offers a variety of food onsite to make sure you've got the energy to carry on all day! There's Woody's Burger Bar for family meal deals and flame grilled burgers; Dixie's Chicken Diner for finger licking southern fried chicken; the Restaurar for pizza, fish and chips an jacket potatoes; Acorn Te Rooms for cream teas an cakes; and a variety of hot do stalls, ice cream kiosks an sweet shops. You can also vis Oakwood's retail shops fo gifts, mementoes and exclusiv ride merchandise – to mak the memories of a great da last!

To make your day easie there's plenty of free parking left luggage facilities, picni areas, baby changing areas an we've even got kennels fo your dog!

Just outside the theme parl is CC2000, Oakwood's indoo bowling and family entertain ment centre. CC2000 is home to a ten-pin bowling alley Games Sector 1 - ar amusement area and the UK': only Crystal Maze game, where you are guided through the Aztec, Medieval, Ocean and Futuristic zones in order tc solve puzzles and collec crystals before entering The Crystal Dome! With a fully-licensed bar and fast food, you can continue the fun unti 11pm.

So fill up on fun at Oakwood!

For a great value family day out call for more information on 01834 861889 or visit our website at www.oakwood-leisure.com

Pembrokeshire
Tourist Information Centres
www.visitpembrokeshire.com

SAUNDERSFOOT TIC
The Harbour, Saundersfoot
Tel: 01834 813672

TENBY TIC
*The Croft, Tenby
Tel: 01834 842404

PEMBROKE VISITOR CENTRE
The Commons Road, Pembroke
Tel: 01646 622388

HAVERFORDWEST TIC
19 Old Bridge, Haverfordwest
Tel: 01437 763110

MILFORD HAVEN TIC
94 Charles Street, Milford Haven
Tel: 01646 690866

PEMBROKE DOCK
Ferry Terminal, Pembroke Dock
Tel: 01646 622753

FISHGUARD TIC
*The Square, Fishguard
Tel: 01348 873484

FISHGUARD HARBOUR TIC
Ocean Lab, Goodwick, Fishguard
Tel: 01348 874737

KILGETTY TIC
Kingsmoor Common, Kilgetty
Tel: 01834 814161

**PEMBROKESHIRE COAST NATIONAL
PARK VISITOR CENTRES**
www.pembrokeshirecoast.org.uk

ST. DAVIDS
The Grove, St. Davids
Tel: 01437 720392

NEWPORT
2 Bank Cottages, Long Street, Newport
Tel: 01239 820912

*It is anticipated that this office may be relocated in 2005,
the telephone number will however remain the same

HAVERFORDWEST & THE WEST COAST

St. Brides

Pembrokeshire's Atlantic West Coast is a wild and dramatic landscape of spectacular cliff scenery, golden beaches and secluded coves. Offshore are the nearby islands of Skomer and Skokholm and, much further out to sea, Grassholm - names which are a reminder of the days when ransacking Viking war lords and Norse settlers made their mark in the area.

This coastline has nothing to compare with Tenby for size and general amenities - a fact which makes it all the more appealing to those visitors in search of peaceful isolation. Even here there are popular village resorts, such as Broad Haven and Dale, which, though small and very relaxing, are only a few miles from the old county town of Haverfordwest and its first-class shopping and other facilities.

Not surprisingly, Haverfordwest has increasingly become a major holiday base for visitors to the Dale Peninsula, Marloes Peninsula, St. Bride's Bay, and even the Preseli Hills. Indeed, it ideally placed for exploring the whole of Pembrokeshire. Close to the major towns and not forgetting the small city of St. Davids.

Even closer to Haverfordwest is the neighbouring town of Milford Haven with its marina and dockside attractions. From here you can catch any of several pleasure boats which ply the Haven waterway to and from Skomer Skokholm and Grassholm. These islands are vitally important habitats for a variety of birds and wildlife. Skomer and Skokholm are best known for their puffins, but they also support the world's largest population of Manx shearwaters. Grassholm has a similar claim to fame; its population of 33,000 pairs of gannets makes it the second largest gannetry in the Northern Hemisphere.

The waters along the coast here are of great environmental importance too. Around Skomer and the Marloes Peninsula is one of only two Marine Nature Reserves in Britain, and the warming influence of the Gulf Stream helps support a rare species of coral. Other marine inhabitants include dolphins, porpoise and Atlantic grey seals.

Map locations: Wolf's Castle, ST. DAVIDS, Nant-y-Coy Mill, Roch, Scolton, Treffgarne, Rudbaxton, HAVERFORDWEST, Newgale, Simpson Cross, Keeston, Nolton Haven, The Rhos, Broad Haven, Picton Castle, Little Haven, St. Ishmaels, MILFORD HAVEN, Marloes, Dale, Llanstadwell, Neyland, PEMBROKE

Another major natural attraction of the remote west is the Pembrokeshire Coastal Path, where walkers can discover the true meaning of solitude. There is a fascinating variety of landscape and geological features to be seen, and the broad sweep of St. Bride's Bay provides a magnificent coastal panorama.

In fact, wherever you choose to stay or by whichever means you choose to explore it, you will soon appreciate that the county's wild west coast presents you with yet a different face of the Pembrokeshire Coast National Park.

HAVERFORDWEST

Distances: Fishguard 16, Milford Haven 7, Narberth 8, Pembroke 11, St. Davids 16, Tenby 19, Carmarthen 30 and London 245.

Haverfordwest, always more English than Welsh and the county town of Pembrokeshire is still the region's most important town, and the biggest centre for shopping and employment.

Overlooking the town centre are the ruins of the medieval castle. The centre itself has a medieval street plan, but first appearances suggest that the only buildings older than late 18th century are the castle and three Norman churches of St.

Mary's, St. Martin's and St. Thomas's. However, behind the new facades of many buildings are much older structures.

The castle was founded prior to 1120 and rebuilt in the 13th century, and only Pembroke was bigger. In 1220 the town was burnt at the hands of Llwelyn the Great, but the castle was undamaged. In 1405 Owain Glyndwr and more than 2,500 men put the town under siege, but again the castle proved impregnable. In the Civil War, Haverfordwest - like Pembroke and Tenby - was held in turn for both King and Parliament, before Cromwell ordered the castle to be slighted in 1648. He also decreed that Haverfordwest should become the county town in place of Pembroke. The keep and substantial sections of wall are all that remain of the castle today, though it has continued to serve the town well over the centuries. In the 18th and 19th centuries it was used as a gaol, until the new county gaol was built in 1820. It has also been a police station.

St. Mary's Church is one of South Wales' finest. Built in the 13th century but substantially altered in the 15th century, it has many outstanding features, including curved oak roofs, a brass dating back to 1651, and an early-English

Marloes Sands

Readers who wish to explore the area are recommended to follow Tour 4 in the Car Tours section.

lancet window. St. Martin's, with its high steeple, is the town's oldest church and has undergone much restoration.

From Tudor times to the early part of this century, Haverfordwest was a flourishing port. Exports included wool, skins, corn, lime and coal, and among the imports were salt, iron, leather, finished goods, and French and Spanish wine. There was a regular if infrequent passenger service to London, which sailed once a month. From the 18th century, many small industries such as limekilns, boatyards, collieries

and quarries sprang up alongside the Western Cleddau and further downstream. Large warehouses lined the quay in Haverfordwest, and the waterway was bustling with fleets of barges, coasting vessels and small steamships. But the decline of the port is a familiar story in 19th-century Wales. In 1853 the arrival of the first train in Haverfordwest was greeted with great celebration. Though this exciting event represented a milestone in the history of the South Wales Railway, it was also the kiss of

Coast &
Country Cottages

COAST & COUNTRY COTTAGES

2005

More choice for 2005, from the Holiday Cottage Specialists

Tel: 01239 881297
www.welsh-cottages.co.uk

Old Bridge,
Haverfordwest

death for the town's maritime trade. A new era in travel had dawned, and shipping could not compete.

Today, the once-hectic quay has become the Riverside Quay Shopping Centre. A modern and attractive development, it includes a large indoor market - a reminder that Haverfordwest has for centuries been an important market town. There is a wide range of fresh local produce on sale here, along with locally made crafts, and a popular open air Farmers Market. There is also a large open-air market held on Sundays on Withybush airfield.

Haverfordwest Town Museum

See Pembrokeshire's Castles and Museums section.

Haverfordwest Sports Centre

See Sporting and Activity section.

Haverfordwest Priory

Robert Fitz-Tancred, castellan of Haverfordwest, who died in 1213, founded the Augustinian Priory of St. Mary & St. Thomas the Martyr. In 1536, during Henry VIII's Dissolution of the Monasteries, it was stripped of its lead roof and the stonework was plundered. Not surprisingly it became a rich source of building stone, but at various times in later years also fulfilled other roles, such as a boatyard, smithy and stables. The ruins, within easy walking distance of the town centre are now being excavated by a team of archaeologists working with CADW (Welsh Historic Monuments), and many interesting finds have been made to date.

Picton Castle

A visit to Picton castle is like no other in Pembrokeshire. A guided tour of a grand historic home gives you a chance to touch a living history that spans more than 750 years, with a highly entertaining journey from the 13th century, through the Civil War, an elegant remodelling in the 1750s and on to the present day.

The history of Picton Castle is all about people and the way they lived. You will hear some fascinating tales of the Philipps family whose home has been at the Castle since the 15th century, and during your tour you will see many fine antiques and paintings.

Then you can soak up the special magic of the grandeur

Scolton Manor

Picton Castle

of the Woodland Gardens as you stroll beneath the largest and some of the oldest trees in West Wales, discovering a feast of wild flowers that blend with beautiful woodland shrubs from all corners of the world.

Unique to Picton are the Rhododendrons raised by their own head gardeners and amongst one of the largest collections of rare species in Wales are Myrtles, Embothrium and Eucryphia.

A walled garden with an elegant fountain and rose strewn arches, displays an enchanting riot of colour in the summer months, and has

medicinal herbs which are labelled with their various remedies.

There's also a maze, a fern walk, a re-landscaped dew pond and even some family fun with a children's nature trail making this a garden visit that can be enjoyed by all ages.

Before you leave you should also visit the old court-yard. This was once the site of the Castle's carpentry shop, the laundry and bakery, but now you will find a Mediterranean style restaurant offering innovative cuisine, a garden nursery that sells many of Picton's rare plants, a gallery that is regular-

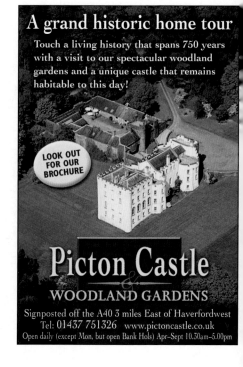

Pembrokeshire County Show

16, 17, 18th August

When the Pembrokeshire Agricultural Society put down its roots permanently on its magnificent Showground at Withybush in the year 1959, few could have foreseen the fantastic growth and development achieved by the County Show during the 46 years since.

The site at Withybush became available for purchase in 1974, and it was a wise and courageous decision by the leaders of the Society to take the plunge and secure the ownership of what has become the finest County Showground in Wales, if not in the whole of the UK.

The Society realised that this was the start of something big. The Show was growing and there was the scope for expansion and opportunities to occupy permanent buildings which today not only houses the various sections for the three days of the Show, but many other events and one day shows are held throughout the year.

Withybush has become the venue of the second best attended agricultural event in the whole of Wales, second only to the Royal Welsh. Attendances have continued to break records with crowds of 100,000 over the three days and with record numbers of livestock and trade stand exhibitions.

Primarily a shop window for agriculture the show also fulfils an educational role and is a thriving centre for business as well.

The 'object' of the Society is the "improvement and encouragement of agriculture" and the organisers' aim is to ensure that everyone going to the show, competitors and visitors, old and young alike, have a good time and enjoy themselves. It's this underlying theme of pleasure and enjoyment that has made the County Show such a popular attraction to the agricultural community and the large number of tourists that visit the County during the summer period. When **the Show opens on Tuesday, 16th August 2005,** visitors can expect to see some 3,800 animals, which includes the cream of Welsh livestock, many of which would have already paraded at the Royal Welsh and Royal England Shows. Avenues will be packed with tradestands displaying the finest and most up-to-date machinery.

The Show has special areas for forestry, conservation, the environment, outdoor pursuits, a huge flower and vegetable exhibition, craft section, and many stands for food, home cooking, bee keeping, poultry fanciers, to mention only a few of the vast array of interests that in essence comprise many small shows within the event.

Visitors to the County should not miss the opportunity of coming to the County Show which has something for everyone.

Newgale

ly used for national art exhibitions and a gift shop that stocks a range individually crafted high quality gifts.

The Castle and Gardens are open from 1st April – 30th September, every day except Mondays. You can visit the Gardens 10.30 – 5.00pm and Castle tours run from 12.00noon – 4.00pm. The gardens remain open in October, 7 days a week, 10.30am – dusk.

For more information ring 01437 751326 or visit their website www.pictoncastle.co.uk

Scolton Heritage Park

Within the park's 60 acres of landscaped grounds and woodland stands Scolton House, which dates back to the 1840's and is furnished throughout in the style of the 1920's. New displays in the Victorian stable block illustrate what life was like on a Pembrokeshire country estate, including stabling, cart shed, carpenter's workshop and smithy.

Other attractions include an animal enclosure arboretum, nature trail and a new 'green' Visitor Centre made entirely of local materials

For more information ring 01437 731328.

Keeston Kitchen, Keeston

A charming country restaurant in Keeston beside the A487 Haverfordwest to St. David's road.

For more information ring 01437 710440.

The Old Smithy

Acquired by Janet & Dario Algieri in early 1998, The Old Smithy at Simpson Cross is one of the oldest stone buildings in the area and was in a poor state of repair. After renovation, it now boasts 2 well lit rooms full of genuine Welsh made crafts and gifts plus a new purpose built gallery displaying the work of at least 14 local artists. Gifts include Welsh Royal Crystal, Pembertons chocolates,

Caldey Island products and the work of three or four local woodturners and carvers, Silver Scenes gifts and much more. There's a large car park shared with the Pembrokeshire Motor Museum, and opposite is the Victorian Conservatory Tea Room making a combined visit to all three a pleasant outing. Seasonal opening plus weekends from mid November through to Christmas for the purchase of ideal local Christmas gifts.

For more information ring 01437 710628 .

THE RHOS

Virtually on the doorstep of this quiet and attractive little village, situated about 2 miles to the south of the main A40 Haverfordwest - St. Clears road, is stately Picton Castle. The road through the village also gives you access to the banks of the Eastern Cleddau - an ideal picnic site on a warm Summer's day. Facing you across the water here is the slipway at Landshipping, and a few hundred yards to your right is Picton Point - the confluence of the Western and Eastern Cleddau rivers.

LITTLE HAVEN

This is a tiny village resort of great charm and beauty, nestling between high cliffs. The beach, a sandy cove which at low tide connects with neighbouring Broad Haven, is popular in summer with bathers and boaters and visitors to its welcoming pubs and restaurants. It is hard to imagine that coal from local pits was once exported from here.

ROCH

Dominating the otherwise flat landscape for miles around, Roch Castle stands on an igneous rock outcrop. The origin of the castle and its large pele tower is unknown, but it is thought that it was built in the 13th century by Adam de Rupe. Legend says that he chose the site because of a prophecy that he would die from an adder's bite. Unluckily for him, an adder was brought into the castle in a bundle of firewood and duly fulfilled the prediction.

The small village of Roch has a 19th-century church with a circular churchyard.

NEWGALE

A popular surfing resort, Newgale is a small village at the northeastern end of St. Bride's Bay, overlooking the impressive 2-mile stretch of Newgale Sands. The sands are separated from the road and village by a high ridge of pebbles. At exceptionally low tides

Little Haven

the stumps of a drowned pre-historic forest are sometimes exposed.

NOLTON HAVEN

This compact coastal village, with its attractive cove, is virtually midway between Little Haven and Newgale. In the 18th century coal was exported from here, and the line of the tramway which brought the anthracite and culm from the mines to the coast can still be seen. Alongside the old track bed is the Counting House, whic[h] recorded how man[y] wagonloads of coal wer[e] transported to the quay. Th[e] quay itself, built in 1769, n[o] longer exists. Half a mil[e] north of Nolton Haven wa[s] Trefran Cliff Colliery, whic[h] worked coal seams beneath St[.] Bride's Bay between 1850 and 1905. Part of an old chimne[y] and other ruins are now th[e] only evidence of this once thriving industry. Th[e] bellcoted church of St[.] Madoc's has a medieval carve[d] stone bracket.

BROAD HAVEN

A favourite beach for bathers since 1800, Broad Haven is the biggest and most popular resort on Pembrokeshire's west coast. The village has good facilities, including guesthouses, a youth hostel, pubs, watersports equipment hire, and plenty of self-catering accommodation, from caravans to cottages. At the northern end of the superb long sandy beach are a number of interesting geological features - folding, stacks and natural arches.

WOLF'S CASTLE

Wolf's Castle (also frequently referred to in print as Wolfscastle) is at the northern end of the Treffgarne Gorge, where in the early part of the century railwaymen toiled to blast an unlikely route through the very old and very hard rock bed in a bid to fulfil Brunel's dream. A motte and bailey castle stands near the centre of the village, which is popular with holidaymakers by virtue of its inn, hotel and pottery.

Archaeological finds nearby include Roman tiles and slates, indicating the site of a fortified Roman-British villa. The village was the birthplace in 1773 of Joseph Harris, who in 1814 published Seren Gomer - the first all-Welsh weekly newspaper.

Milford Haven

TREFFGARNE

Treffgarne was the birthplace (c1359) of the rebellious Welsh hero Owain Glyndwr. The village stands close to the wooded rocky gorge, through which runs the Western Cleddau river, railway line and main A40 trunk road. The Treffgarne Gorge was cut by meltwater rushing south towards Milford Haven during the retreat of the last Ice Age. The areas around the gorge are dotted with sites of early settlements and fortifications, and on the western side rises the igneous outcrop of Great Treffgarne Mountain and other striking rock formations.

Nant-y-Coy Mill

Restored Nant-y-Coy Mill dates back to 1332 and possibly even earlier. The last corn was ground here in the 1950's, but the mill wheel is still turning - 150 years after it was built. The mill is a very attractive crafts centre, museum and tea room, with a nature trail leading up to Great Treffgarne Rocks, from where the views of the gorge are spectacular. You can also take a detour to Lion Rock and Bear Rock - two of the most distinctive features of the Pembrokeshire landscape.

The mill's wide selection of quality craft products is displayed on two floors, made all the more interesting by the inclusion of items relating to local history. The tearoom, mill wheel and ground floor of the craft centre and museum has wheelchair access.

The mill has been closed for refurbishment, and hope to be open again in the Summer of 2005. Tel: 0143? 741671 for further details, or check our website for progress www.nantycoy.co.uk

RUDBAXTON

Rudbaxton is about 2 miles north of Haverfordwest and is the site of one of the region's most impressive earthworks - a motte and bailey fortress established in the 11th century. In a valley below the mound is the parish church of St. Michael. This dates from the 12th century and was restored in the 1870's.

MILFORD HAVEN

Distances: Fishguard 24, Haverfordwest 7, Narberth 15, Pembroke 7, St. Davids 21, Tenby 17, Carmarthen 37 and London 253.

Since its development as a new town and whaling port in the late 18th century, Milford Haven has seen its economic fortunes seesaw. Sir William Hamilton, husband of Nelson's Emma, was granted an Act of Parliament to proceed with the development of the town and port, and from the beginning it was envisaged that new Milford would secure

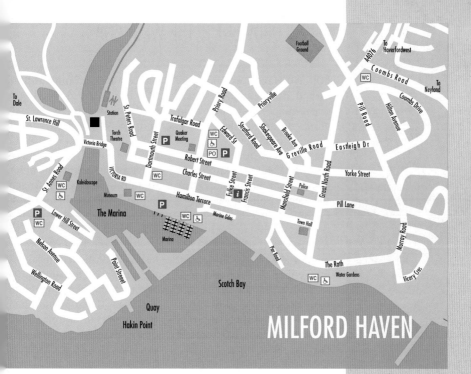

MILFORD HAVEN

its share of the transatlantic shipping trade.

Assisted by settlers from overseas, progress was rapid, with the early establishment of a quay, custom house, inn and naval dockyard. When Nelson visited in 1802 he was suitably impressed with the development and the Haven waterway, which he described as 'one of the world's finest natural harbours'.

However, it was not long before the town's development suffered major setbacks. Whaling at the port ceased, and in 1814 the Admiralty transferred the naval dockyard several miles east to Paterchurch (now Pembroke Dock) - despite the fact that many fine ships had been built at Milford Haven in a very short space of time.

Another setback followed when, in 1836, the daily Irish Packet boat service was also moved from Milford to Paterchurch.

During the mid-1800's, a renewed effort was made to re-establish Milford Haven as a trans-Atlantic staging post and ambitious plans were drawn up for the building of docks to rival those at Liverpool and Southampton. Although these never materialised, the far more modest Milford Haven docks opened in 1888.

New life was breathed into the new docks when the first vessel to enter was the steam trawler Sybil on 27th September 1888. Her arrival marked the beginning of a prosperous new era for

Milford Haven as the port turned its attention to deep-sea fishing. The combination of new docks, excellent fishing grounds and good rail links saw the enterprise reap rich rewards. Milford Haven thus became one of Britain's most successful fishing ports.

In its heyday in the 1920's the port was home to 130 deep sea trawlers which offered employment to around 4,000 men either afloat or ashore.

By the 1950's the seesaw had tipped the other way again as the fishing industry slipped into an irretrievable decline. This time, however, the promise of yet another new beginning for Milford Haven was already in the pipeline: the coming of the oil industry.

The oil companies were attracted to West Wales for a number of reasons. Of major consideration was the sheltered deep-water anchorage offered by the Haven waterway, which could accommodate crude oil tankers of ever-increasing size. The local authorities also made it clear they welcomed the new industry, pointing out the availability of a large labour pool.

In recent years this industry too has had its ups and downs. The rising cost of crude oil in the 1970's and 1980's saw many refineries in Europe close, and a subsequent slimming down of the

oil business around Milford Haven resulted in the closure of the Esso refinery in 1983 and the BP ocean terminal in 1985.

Now only one refinery remains, but despite the industry's problems the wealth generated by oil has helped fund Milford Haven's massive new investment in tourism. This has seen the complete refurbishment of the old docks and the creation of the superb 150-berth marina. Many old buildings have been demolished, while others of historic significance have been renovated and now house such attractions as the museum. A thriving retail and business park has been developed which has attracted many new businesses to the Docks area. The old shopping centre has been attractively remodelled, and the town's gardens and esplanade upgraded and landscaped to reflect their Victorian heritage. In addition, leisure facilities are first-class.

Milford Marina

Since it so successfully hosted the start of the 1991 Cutty Sark Tall Ships Race, Milford Marina has seen visitors returning in large numbers. There is an excellent variety of places to eat, to suit all tastes and budgets, an adventure playground for younger visitors

Milford Marina

and recently opened ten-pin bowling centre.

For more information about Milford Marina ring 01646 692272 (24 hr).

Phoenix Bowl

Offering entertainment and fun regardless of age or ability, Phoenix Bowl is one of Milford Marina's most recent and lively attractions. Whether it be for a hectic, action-packed family day out, or for a quiet lunch overlooking the busy, yet picturesque Dock of Milford Haven, this ten-pin bowling Centre has become a popular venue for locals and tourists alike.

Along with a sophisticated ten-lane set-up, the Centre also boasts a separate pool-room and Pirate Pete's Soft Play Area.

If this all sounds a little too active and spectating is more in your league, then enjoy the action from the comfort of the fully licensed bar, that is now complete with 'big-screen' coverage of major sporting events.

The Centre also encompasses a highly acclaimed restaurant that has a growing reputation and varied menu.

Open 10.00am - 11.00pm daily.

For more information ring 01646 696350.

Welsh Marine Life Rescue & Seal Hospital

A rescue and rehabilitation centre for seals and other marine mammals, run by a team of dedicated volunteers. Visitors are welcome.

For more information ring 01646 692943.

Milford Haven Museum

Housed in the Old Custom House of 1797, this fascinating museum tells the story of Charles Francis Greville, who supervised the development of Milford into a new town and port two centuries ago, and of the American whalers from Nantucket who settled here. It also recalls the days in the port's history when trawlers and drifters filled the docks

Below: Welsh Marine Life Rescue and Seal Hospital at Milford Haven

and 'every day was pay day' and relates Milford's role in two world wars and the arrival of the oil industry with its multi-million-pound refineries. *For more information ring 01646 694496.*

Torch Theatre

The Torch Theatre in Milford Haven, is one of only three professional building-based producing theatres in the whole of Wales. In 2002 the Torch celebrated its Silver Jubilee with an award-winning production of One Flew Over the Cuckoo's Nest directed by Peter Doran. The Torch Theatre Company's impressive repertoire of productions include: The Woman in Black, Neville's Island, Abigail's Party, Blue Remembered Hills, Little Shop of Horrors, The Caretaker, Of Mice and Men, Educating Rita and Bedroom Farce plus many more – all of which have played to critical acclaim from local and national press. The Torch's annual Christmas Musical production is a family favourite, featuring original script (Peter Doran) and music composed by James Williams.

The Theatre holds 297 seats, and as well as productions from the Torch Theatre Company, the venue hosts visiting productions from companies and celebrities; provides a cinema facility; is home to the Joanna Field Art Gallery; houses the Torch Sound Studio (with resident professional musicians & composers); is home to the Torch Youth Theatre & Education Department - running education-linked activities for all members of the local and wider community and provides a useful space for a range of community groups to meet (eg amateur drama and art societies).

Come to the Torch and find out why we're known as Pembrokeshire's Premier Arts Venue.

To find out more about what's on, please call our Box Office on 01646 695267, check our ads in the local press, call in and pick up a brochure or visit www.torchtheatre.co.uk.

Milford Leisure Centre

Popular multi-purpose leisure centre with swimming pool, fitness suite and indoor bowls.

See Activity Section.

NEYLAND

Like Milford Haven, Neyland has been revitalised by the building of an impressive new marina and waterfront development - Brunel Quay. Its name could only be a reference to the great railway engineer, whose aim was to establish Neyland as a prosperous transatlantic port by choosing it as the

The award-winning Torch Theatre in Pembrokeshire offers something for everyone, from the best live theatre shows to latest cinema releases and monthly exhibitions in the Joanna Field Art Gallery.

Torch Theatre Box Office: 01646 695267
To join our free mailing list, please contact Maria on 01646 694192.
Visit our website at **www.torchtheatre.co.uk**

Above:
Torch Theatre production
of "Blue Remembered Hills"

Right:
Torch Theatre production
of "Of Mice and Men"

terminus of the South Wales Railway. An impressive statue of Brunel now stands at the entrance to Brunel Quay in recognition of his achievements. (At one time or other during the 18th and 19th centuries, virtually every port and resort on the entire Welsh coast had designs on winning the battle for the highly lucrative transatlantic trade. Sadly, none of them ever succeeded.)

In the event, Neyland was not to realise this grand ambition, but until 1906 the town did become an important terminus for the Irish ferries. In that year the service was transferred to Fishguard in the north of the county. But the railway remained operational until 1964, when the town's depot was closed.

The route of the old railway line now provides an enjoyable country walk between the marina and the village of Rosemarket. Mountain bikers can also tackle the 14-mile circular Brunel Cycle Route.

The 380-berth marina itself occupies the site where Brunel's depot and quay once stood, and in the last few years has established Neyland as a major sailing and watersports centre. Alongside the marina are attractive new homes and a popular waterside cafe and bar. The redevelopment scheme has also created a fine promenade and picnic area, with superb views of the Cleddau Bridge and the busy waterway.

LLANSTADWELL

Just west of Neyland along the Haven shoreline, the small hillside village of Llanstadwell overlooks the estuary and Pembroke Dock, in the shadow of the former Gulf's Waterston refinery.

There are some pretty cottages here, and the medieval parish church enjoys a picturesque position. The village inn and restaurant is a popular retreat.

ST. ISHMAELS

Located between Milford Haven and Dale, the village of St. Ishmael's lies in a deep sheltered valley. Nearby are important historic sites - a Norman motte and bailey to the north, and the Iron Age forts of Great and Little Castle Heads to the east.

The 12th-century church stands away from the village, on the site where St. Ishmael is believed to have founded his principal church in the 6th century.

A stream divides the churchyard.

DALE

The seaside village of Dale enjoys a sheltered position on the northern shoreline of the Haven waterway, close to the entrance at St. Ann's Head. This one-time shipbuilding and trading port is now one of the most popular sailing centres in Pembrokeshire, and has good facilities for visitors. Races are held on most days during the summer, and in August there is a regatta.

Close to the village is Dale Fort, one of the Victorian defences built to protect the waterway, and now used as a geographical field study centre. At the western end of the village, the road leads to the magnificent headland of St. Ann's Head, with its lighthouse and coastguard station from where there are stunning views of the Haven waterway and its busy shipping lanes.

MARLOES

This pretty little village with its attractive cottages and church lies

Dale

en-route to Marloes Sands, off the B4327. Marloes Sands can be reached from the village or from Dale. The panoramic views from the cliffs above the superb beach take in the islands of Skomer, Skokholm and the much smaller Grassholm, which at low tide can be reached from the northern end of the beach. The road through Marloes village also gives you access to the peaceful cove of Martin's Haven - the departure point for Skomer Island and other island boat trips.

Above:
St Brides

Top:
Marloes Sands

WHERE to eat out

HAVERFORDWEST & THE WEST COAST

KEESTON
Keeston Kitchen
*A mouthwatering selection of home-cooked food
and excellent wine in friendly surroundings*

HAVERFORDWEST
McDonalds Restaurant
Good fast food for the whole family!   *see page no. 49*

BROAD HAVEN
Nautilus
*A popular bar & restaurant with function rooms.
Outstanding food in a stylish contemporary setting
with stunning seafront and sunset views*   *see page no. 83*

ST. DAVIDS & THE NORTH COAST

PORTHGAIN
The Sloop Inn
*A varied menu catering for all tastes and
only 100 yards from the harbour*   *see page no. 105*

MATHRY
The Farmers Arms
*Charming old inn serving good home made food
in the bar or conservatory garden room*   *see page no. 106*

TREFIN
Oriel-y-Felin Gallery & Tearoom
*Mouthwatering lunches, clotted cream teas, etc.,
using the best of Pembrokeshire produce*   *see page no. 107*

CASTLE MORRIS
Tides Restaurant & Coffee Shop
*Exciting menu featuring wholesome dishes and
situated at Llangloffan Farm, famous for its
traditional Welsh farmhouse cheeses*   *see page no. 115*

WHERE to eat out

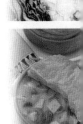

MOYLEGROVE

Pavilion Cafe, Penrallt Nursery & Garden Centre

Enjoy home-made lunches, freshly made coffee and wonderful cream teas, set in a beautiful location overlooking the sea at Ceibwr Bay.

see page no. 118

INLAND PEMBROKESHIRE

CLARBESTON ROAD

Llys-y-fran Reservoir Restaurant/Tea Rooms

Restaurant menu and beverages available whilst you visit the Reservoir

see page no. 123

ROSEBUSH

The Old Post Office Tea Rooms & Restaurant

Good Welsh cooking from local produce

BONCATH

The Nags Head

Historic riverside pub well known for its superb pub food, interesting restaurant menu and generous portions

CLYNDERWEN

Trefach Country Pub

Restaurant and fully licensed bar open all year round

see page no. 125

NARBERTH

The Creative Café

Paint your own pottery whilst enjoying special coffees, baguettes and home made cakes

see page no. 134

If you wish to be included in our next "Where to eat" section of this guide then please telephone us on 01646 682296 for further details.

The magnificent Harrison and Harrison Org
of St Davids Cathedr

Photo: Mr C.R.A. Davies, LR

ST DAVIDS & THE NORTH COAST

Compared with Tenby and the more developed south, North Pembrokeshire is better known for its rugged beauty and ancient landscape than for its leisure attractions and amusements. Yet many of the features which annually bring hundreds of thousands of visitors to the area can be described truthfully as manmade - some as long ago as 5000 years.

The sights awaiting those visitors with a will to explore are as fascinating as they are varied. They include such delights as the cathedral and city of St. Davids; the superb beach of Whitesands; the picturesque village and harbour of Solva; small coastal resorts such as Abereiddy and Porthgain; the golden sands of Newport. There are also traditional crafts and Welsh industries such as cheese making as well as working woollen mills; together with the historic port of Fishguard.

Inland, the beautiful Gwaun Valley and rolling Preseli Hills add their own mystique to a landscape liberally endowed with prehistoric sites and ancient burial chambers.

To the Welsh, the greatest saint of all was of course St. David - the patron saint of Wales. The spectacularly beautiful peninsula which bears his name is the most hallowed spot in the country, for this was his reputed birthplace. It was here that he established a semi-monastic religious settlement in around 550. This site is now occupied by the famous 12th-century cathedral which gives the village of St. Davids its entitlement to city status. It is the

Top: Whitesands Bay
Above: Solva

Overlooking Whitesands, St. Davids

smallest city in Britain; some sources claim it to be the smallest in the world.

The skyline is dominated not by the tower of St. Davids Cathedral, as you might expect, but by stark hills of igneous rock such as Carn Llidi. If anything the cathedral is conspicuous by its absence, because until you are in its immediate vicinity it is very effectively hidden in the vale of the tiny River Alun.

Carn Llidi is deceptive to the eye. It rises a modest 600 feet above sea level, but looks much higher. It was because of the unprecedented views to the west and north that Carn Llidi proved strategically useful in both world wars. In

the first it bore a hydrophon station for detecting sub marines; in the second it wa the site for a lookout and radar installation.

Near Carn Llidi, and over looked by St. Davids Head, i Whitesands Bay. This super beach, very popular in summe is the best in Nort Pembrokeshire and has beer described as the best in Wales.

South of Whitesands Bay i an expanse of countryside - ar ancient agricultural landscape of fertile soils and arable fields Further south still, the ruins o St. Justinian's Chapel stand near the little cove o Porthstinian, which is also the home of the St. Davids Lifeboa Station. This was built in 1869.

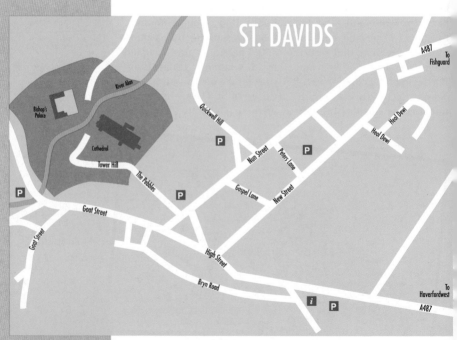

ST. DAVIDS

Distances: Fishguard 16, Haverfordwest 16, Milford Haven 21, Narberth 25, Pembroke 26, Tenby 35, Carmarthen 46 and London 266.

St. Davids is living proof that size is not important. As any visitor will quickly discover, the cathedral city is in reality a modest but very charming village. People still flock here in their thousands, as they did throughout the Middle Ages when this was a place of pilgrimage, and the cathedral remains the major object of attention. Yet impressive and hugely significant though it is, the cathedral is small by English standards and because it is hidden in a sheltered valley you could pass through St. Davids without even knowing that Wales' greatest religious monument is here.

The village-cum-city dates back to the 6th century and stands about a mile from the sea, on a wide plateau overlooking the diminutive River Alun. The centre of St. Davids is marked by Cross Square, so called because of its restored ancient cross. High Street is something of a misnomer for the road which runs in from Solva and Haverfordwest, but it does contain City Hall.

Inevitably all roads lead to the 12th-century cathedral. Less well known, but no less impressive, are the ruins of the once-magnificent Bishop's

St. Davids

St. Davids Lifeboat Station

97

Palace, which stand opposite the cathedral in Cathedral Close. The Close is an area of 18 acres, lying below the village in the vale of the River Alun. It is believed that this secluded site was chosen for the original 6th-century church so that it would not be visible from the sea to passing pirates and raiders, who frequently made it their business to ransack western coastal communities and pilfer whatever treasures the churches and chapels might contain. However, the ploy failed; Vikings burnt the church no less than eight times during the centuries leading up to the Norman Conquest.

The path from the village down to Cathedral Close takes you through the 13th-century Tower Gate - one of four gatehouses which formed part of the Close's precinct wal Within the Close stands th cathedral, the Bishop's Palac and various other ecclesiast cal buildings, including th houses of church dignitaries At this point you are still abov the level of the cathedral, an to reach it requires a furthe descent of a flight of thirty nine steps (no connectior with John Buchan) known a the Thirty-Nine Articles. Th Cathedral and Bishop's Palac are marvels of medieval archi tecture, all the more strikin; for the remarkable tranquillit of this remote setting.

St. Davids Cathedral

The cathedral as it stand: today was begun in 1180 by Peter de Leia, the third Norman bishop, and completed in 1522. In 1220 the central tower collapsed - an occurrence apparently no

The Bell Tower

unknown in medieval churches - and further damage was inflicted by a severe earthquake in 1248. Early in the 14th century, Bishop Gower (nicknamed the building bishop' because of his love for creating great buildings) carried out many changes and improvements to the cathedral. He raised the walls of the aisles, inserted the decorated and much larger windows, built the south porch and transept chapels, and vaulted the Lady Chapel. In around 1340 he also built the Bishop's Palace to accommodate the large numbers of pilgrims visiting the cathedral. The palace, a structure of such splendour that even the ruins are impressive, stands opposite the cathedral.

As the cathedral expanded, an increasing number of clerical residences and other ecclesiastical buildings grew up around it, and a wall with gatehouses was built to protect the community. The last of the great builders to contribute to the cathedral was Bishop Vaughan, who in the early 16th century raised the tower to its present height and built the perpendicular chapel dedicated to the Holy Trinity.

Following the Reformation the cathedral was neglected. The roof of the Lady Chapel was stripped of its lead and subsequently - though much later - collapsed. Severe damage was also inflicted in the Civil War. In 1862 Sir George Gilbert Scott was commissioned to begin a complete restoration of the cathedral, and not surprisingly the work continued into this century. In 1866, during the restoration, the bones of two men were found in a recess which had been walled up. It is believed that these were the remains of St. David and his friend and teacher, St. Justinian. They are now contained in an oak chest in the Holy Trinity chapel. Other tombs in the cathedral include those of Bishop Gower, Edmund Tudor - father of Henry VII - and Giraldus Cambrensis.

St. Davids Cathedral, which is open to visitors every day, is the largest church in Wales, and certainly the most interesting. The total interior length is nearly 300 feet and the tower is 125 ft high: small by comparison with cathedrals on the grand scale of York Minster, but a mighty inspiration to the Welsh for centuries past and, no doubt, for centuries to come.

Bishop's Palace

This grand and richly decorated palace was largely the work of Bishop Henry de Gower, who also left his very distinctive mark on Lamphey Bishop's Palace and Swansea Castle. It was built mainly between 1328 and 1347, and stands opposite the cathedral

Readers who wish to explore the area are recommended to follow Tour 6 in the Car Tours section.

*Cross Square,
St. Davids*

in Cathedral Close, amongst a group of medieval buildings unique in Wales. The palace played host to many pilgrims, whose numbers included monks, bishops and kings. Even in ruin, the battlements, curtain walls, gatehouse and entrance to the Great Hall are impressive, and of particular interest are Bishop Gower's arcaded parapets, which are decorated with some of the finest examples of medieval sculptured heads and animals to be found in Wales.

The Bishop's Palace houses two fascinating exhibitions - Life in the Palace of a Prince of the Church and Lords of the Palace - it is also the venue for a number of special events. These include performances of Shakespeare plays and a December carol service. The palace is in the care of CADW (Welsh Historic Monuments) and is open every day except Christmas Eve, Christmas Day, Boxing Day and New Year's Day.

For more information including details of special events, ring 01437 720517 or 02920 500200.

St. Davids Cathedral Festival

The Cathedral has a long tradition going back to the famous composer Thomas Tompkins, who was born in

St. Davids in 1572, the son of the then cathedral organist. In the autumn of 2000, Dr Roy Massey, Hereford Cathedral's Organist and Master of the Choristers, gave the inaugural recital of the Cathedral's splendid Father Willis organ, newly restored by Harrison and Harrison and now displayed in a magnificent new case on the Nave Screen.

It is one of the remarkable facts of Britain's smallest city that despite a scant population and no choir school foundation, St. Davids can proudly boast three outstanding cathedral choirs, whose presence will again bring great harmony to the Cathedral Music Festival, founded in 1979.

The Festival provides an excellent opportunity to experience the pleasures of the beautiful Pembrokeshire Coast National Park by day, with music making in the evening by some of the world's top musicians in one of the most historic and revered buildings in Wales. In 2005 this 26th annual celebration of classical music takes place between 28th May and 5th June.

For more information check out the Festival's website: www.stdavidscathedral.org.uk or contact the Festival Administrator on 01437 721682 or via Email: festival@tretio.net

St. Non's Chapel (St. Non's Bay)

Non was the mother of David, the man destined to become the patron saint of Wales. Standing in a field above St. Non's Bay, just south of St. Davids, the original ruined chapel is reputedly the oldest Christian monument in Wales. It is also said to mark the exact spot where St. David was born in the 6th century, during a thunderstorm. Near the chapel is a holy well that miraculously appeared at the moment of birth. In the Middle Ages the well attracted many people who came to cure their ailments. The present St. Non's Chapel was built in 1934.

PORTHCLAIS

In centuries past, this picturesque inlet was a busy little harbour - the port of the monastic community at St. Davids. Its sheltered anchorage saw the comings and goings of countless monks, priests, pilgrims, Norman soldiers, pirates, and even kings. Purple stone from nearby Caerfai and Caerbwdy was landed here to help build the cathedral, along with Irish oak for the roof of the nave.

Trade thrived here in the Tudor and Stuart periods, with exports of cereal to the West Country. Later years saw the import of limestone to feed the four kilns on the quayside, two of which have been restored.

Above: Porthclais
Below: Bishop's Palace, St. Davids

ST DAVIDS & THE NORTH COAST

Porthstinian

ST. JUSTINIAN'S

The name actually refers to the remains of St. Justinian's Chapel, but over time it has become synonymous with the little creek and harbour of Porthstinian. The presence of the chapel recalls the legend of St. Justinian, who founded a small religious community on nearby Ramsey Island. But the discipline he imposed on his followers was so strict that they rebelled and cut off his head, whereupon St. Justinian picked it up, walked over the sea to the mainland, laid down his head and died.

PORTHSTINIAN

Porthstinian is well known as the home of the St. Davids lifeboat station. This was founded in 1868, though it was 1912 before the buildings and slipway were built. The rocky coastline and dangerous offshore reefs, such as the Smalls and the Bishops and Clerks, make this an extremely treacherous area for seaborne traffic, and the lifeboats which have seen service here have been involved in many dramatic rescues.

Porthstinian has a beach but is unsuitable for bathing. Just across the water is Ramsey Island, separated from the mainland by hazardous Ramsey Sound.

Middle Mill, Solva

SOLVA

Without question this must be one of the most charming and attractive coastal villages in Britain. Just east of St. Davids on the A487 Haverfordwest road, Solva is a beautiful rocky inlet which floods except at low tide, so providing a sheltered, safe anchorage for yachts and pleasure craft.

Not surprisingly, this fine natural harbour has given the village a long seafaring tradition. Shipbuilding and maritime trade flourished here until the railway arrived in Pembrokeshire in the middle of the 19th century. In its heyday the busy port had a thriving import and export business, nine warehouses, twelve limekilns, a direct passenger service to New York, and also played an important role in the construction of the two remote lighthouses erected at different times on the Smalls - a treacherous cluster of jagged rocks lurking 21 miles off Pembrokeshire's west coast.

The facts relating to the passenger service to New York are a particularly fascinating slice of Solva's history. In 1848 the one-way fare for an adult was £3. For this you were sure of a bed space but had to take your own food - and the voyage could take anything from 7 to 17 weeks!

The most popular part of this favourite holiday village, which is split into two, is Lower Solva, with its harbour, surviving limekilns and a charming selection of shops, pubs and restaurants.

Solva is an excellent place to join the Pembrokeshire Coastal Path, as the cliff scenery on either side of the inlet is magnificent. If you just fancy an easy stroll you can walk along the harbour, or take the footpath above the opposite (eastern) side of the inlet. This takes you to the top of the Gribin - a strip of land between two valleys - where you can see the site of an Iron Age settlement and superb views of the village an harbour..

MIDDLE MILL

Just north of Solva, a mile up the valley of the river of the same name nestles the attrac-

tive little waterside hamlet of Middle Mill. Here you will find a working woollen mill, which opened in 1907 and has been in production ever since. This family-run business invites you to watch the process that turns the finest Welsh wool into a range of high-quality rugs, tweeds, carpets and clothes, all of which are for sale on the premises.

ABEREIDDY

An attractive west-facing bay on the north coast of the St. Davids Peninsula, Abereiddy is famous locally for its striking Blue Lagoon - once a slate quarry linked to the sea by a narrow channel but closed in 1904 after it was flooded during a storm. The lagoon is now considered an important geological feature, and the quarry yields many fossils. The coastal scenery between here and St. Davids

Solva

103

Llanrhian Church

Head is outstanding. To the north there are traces of the old narrow-gauge railway track which once took the quarried slate and shale to the harbour at nearby Porthgain for export.

Abereiddy is about two miles east of Croesgoch, on the A487 St. Davids-Fishguard road.

Pembrokeshire Sheepdogs

On the beautiful north coast of Pembrokeshire, close to St. Davids is Tremynydd Fach Farm, home of Pembrokeshire Sheepdogs Training Centre. The centre runs courses for owners and handlers and their dogs from novice to advanced stages training right up to 'One Man and His Dog' standard.

However, for the casual visitor they also run demonstrations throughout the season which allow everyone to watch a wonderful exhibition of the skills of working dogs.

From the youngest pups just beginning to show the instinct for their work through all stages of training to dogs of three to four years at the height of their skills, all can be seen working sheep (and other animals!) and clearly having a great time doing it. There's also a surprise finale.

Teas and home cooked cakes at extremely reasonable prices, plus the opportunity to talk to the handlers, make this a wonderful insight into working dogs and a thoroughly enjoyable afternoon for all ages. Delightful circular walk through fields and along the coastal path. You can even bring your own dog to watch - on his lead please.

Ring 01437 721677 for demonstration times.

LLANRHIAN

Llanrhian is a hamlet standing at a crossroads on the road between Croesgoch and Porthgain. It is notable because of the unusual parish church, dedicated to St. Rhian, which is cruciform in shape and has a number of interesting features including a 15th-century ten-sided font. Also striking is the tall tower, built in the 13th century. The rest of the church was completely rebuilt in 1836 and restored in 1891.

PORTHGAIN

A small hamlet in the parish of Llanrhian, Porthgain is one of the most individual places in Pembrokeshire, with superb coastal scenery and an unpretentious mixture of traditional, Victorian and later

The Blue Lagoon, Abereiddy (top); Porthgain

Top: Abercastle

style houses, and a man-made 19th Century harbour. The harbour was once a hive of activity and its reconstruction between 1902 and 1904 to make way for larger quays reflected its significant shipping activities. These included the exportation of slate and shale from the quarry at Abereiddy and bricks made from local clay, mainly for local use.

The main export however was the medium to fine granite stone; exceptionally hard and used for the construction of buildings and roads as far apart as Liverpool, Dublin and London. Porthgain was a village whose

employment was entirely dependent on the prosperity of the quarry and by the turn of the century, the company known as 'Porthgain Village Industries Ltd' boasted a fleet of nearly 100 vessels including six steam coasters of 350 tons each. Even as late as 1931, the harbour was improved for hoped for 170ft 650 ton ships to enter, but after the First World War this maritime trade went into decline, as it did all over Britain due to the slump and by 1931 had ceased production entirely. In 1983 the Pembrokeshire Coast National Park Authority acquired the attractive harbour, and the remains of the buildings bear testimony to Porthgain's industrial past.

Porthgain remains a very lively community with a flourishing tourist trade due to it's magnificent stretch of coastline and many significant antiquarian remains, making it a must-see for those interested in either industrial archaeology or ancient history, while a couple of miles north-east of Porthgain lies a fine Iron Age fort called Castell Coch. Porthgain is well worth a visit for its diversity of interest. One of Britain's finest geographers described the coast between Porthgain and Abereiddy as the finest in Britain. Today, fish are still regularly landed at Porthgain harbour.

The Sloop Inn at Porthgain is probably one of the best-

Trefin

nown pubs in the area. The pub dates back to 1743, when it was more a workers than walkers pub. Nowadays, the Sloop makes a welcome stop for those walking along the coastal path. The premises offer good parking and space for children to play together with a large picnic area.

MATHRY

The village of Mathry stands on a hill just off the A487 between St. Davids and Fishguard, a few miles east of Trefin. Its elevated position gives superb coastal views, and of particular interest here is the parish church. This unusual squat building and circular churchyard occupy a prehistoric site, possibly dating from the Iron Age. At one time the church had a steeple that served as a landmark for mariners. Like Trefin, the village is a popular watering hole for visitors passing through. Just west of Mathry is the site of an ancient burial chamber.

TREFIN

Just to the east of Porthgain and its attractive harbour, Trefin is the largest coastal village between St. Davids and Fishguard. It is close to a shingle and sand beach known as Aber Felin, and the proximity of the coast path makes this a popular watering hole for walkers. It is worth noting that disabled visitors can gain easy access to this section of the coast path. There is also a youth hostel in the village. Near the shoreline stands the ruin of Trefin Mill, which closed in 1918 and has been partly restored by the National Park Authority. The mill was immortalised in the famous Welsh poem Melin Trefin.

Above: "Farm above Aberfelin" by Pauline Beynon at Oriel-Y-Felin Gallery

Top: Goodwick

Right:
View from Garn Fawr

ABERCASTLE

Abercastle stands on Pembrokeshire's rocky northern coastline, southwest of Strumble Head and close to the villages of Trefin and Mathry. From the 16th century onwards this was a busy little coastal port, at various times in its history involved in the export of corn, butter and oats and the import of general goods, anthracite, culm and limestone. The limekiln still survives on the attractive harbour. Abercastle can claim a small piece of important maritime history: in 1876 the first man to sail solo across the Atlantic landed here.

Half a mile west of the village, standing just off the coast path, is Carreg Samson - an excellent example of a Bronze Age burial chamber.

The capstone is 15 feet long and 9 feet wide, and according to legend Samson placed it in position using only his little finger.

GOODWICK

Until the harbour was completed in 1906, Goodwick was nothing more than a cluster of fishermen's cottages. But as the new terminus for the main railway line from London, this one-time village quickly adopted the status of a major ferry port and today is still the link between Fishguard and Rosslare in Ireland. Inevitably, Goodwick has grown so close, in every sense, to its very near neighbour Fishguard that it is now virtually a suburb of the larger town and the two are synonymous.

PUBLIC
FOOTPATH

36th FISHGUARD INTERNATIONAL MUSIC FESTIVAL
Saturday 23rd to Saturday 30th July 2005

BBC National Orchestra of Wales
conductor - Paul Watkins,

Nash Ensemble
Allegri String Quartet
The National Youth String Academy

The John S. Davies Singers
and the Female Voices of the
John S. Davies Singers
Côr Dewi Sant
Westward Chamber Orchestra
leader - David Juritz
conductor - John S. Davies

Martin Roscoe *piano* - Paul Watkins *cello*
Katona Twins - *guitar duo*
Matthew Trusler - *violin*
Ieuan Jones - *harp*

Live Music Now! - *young artists*

Details (all year round)
Festival Office, Fishguard, Pembs SA65 9BJ
Tel/fax. 01348-873612   Email: fishguard-imf@cwcom.net

FISHGUARD

Distances: Haverfordwest 16, Milford Haven 22, Narberth 24, Pembroke 26, Tenby 35, Carmarthen 46 and London 272.

Fishguard and Goodwick, 16 miles northeast of St. Davids, are the only parts of Pembrokeshire's outer coastline which are not within the National Park. But they are certainly no less attractive for that, offering a good choice of accommodation and an ideal base for discovering all that this part of the county has to show you.

The harbour is in fact the main sailing centre of the North Pembrokeshire coast. Before the harbour was built, Fishguard had established itself as a very busy port, with slate, corn, butter and cured pilchards and herrings representing the main exports. During the 18th century only Haverfordwest was handling a greater volume of trade. Shipbuilding was important too; the shipyard was renowned for its schooners and square-rigged vessels.

The harbour and impressive breakwater on the Goodwick side of the bay were built in 1906 to attract the transatlantic liners away from Liverpool and Southampton. But as was the reality for Milford Haven, Cardigan, New Quay and other hopeful West Wales ports, the big dream did not materialise. However, there was compensation in successfully establishing the ferry links with Ireland - a lasting and positive return on the massive task of constructing the breakwater, which consumed 800 tons of rock along every foot of its half-mile length!

Fishguard has remained a major British ferry port with excellent port facilities. However, its biggest contribution to the history books occurred on 22nd February 1797, when the town was the scene of an extraordinary invasion which has the distinction of being the last invasion of British soil.

The uninvited guests were members of a French expeditionary force under the command of an American-Irish adventurer, Colonel William Tate, who had a commission in the French army. His mission was to seize Bristol - at that time Britain's second city - but bad weather forced the

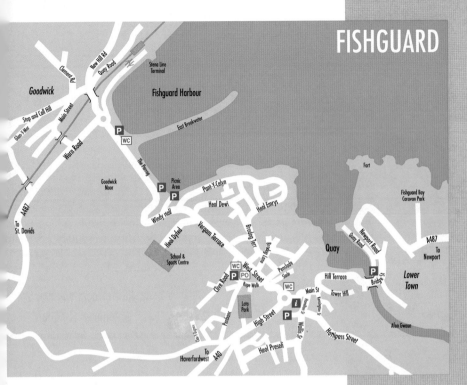

Goodwick

Fishguard Harbour

Stena Line Terminal

New Hill Rd

Quay Road

Clement Rd

Main Street

Stop and Call Hill

Glan-y-Mor

Wern Road

A487

To St. Davids

Goodwick Moor

The Parrog

East Breakwater

Picnic Area

Windy Hall

Heol Dyfed

Pant-Y-Celyn

Heol Dewi

Vergam Terrace

Heol Emrys

School & Sports Centre

Clive Road

West Street

PO

Rope Walk

Loto Park

Pendant

High Street

Brodog Terr

Brodog Lane

Pembroke Slade

Main St

Kensington St

Tower Hill

Wallis Sq

Heol Preseli

Heol Preseli

To Haverfordwest

A40

Quay

Hill Terrace

Bridge

Lower Town

Afon Gwaun

Hamilton St

Hortipass Street

Fort

Fishguard Bay Caravan Park

Newport Road

Quay Road

A487

To Newport

ships to land at Carreg Wastad Point, northwest of Fishguard. Once ashore, Tate's troops set about pilfering farms and homesteads, gorging themselves with as much food as they could lay their hands on, washed down with barrels of spirit which the local people had salvaged from a recent shipwreck. In this somewhat unfit condition the soldiers approached the town and, according to local tradition, mistook a crowd of women in red shawls and tall hats for guardsmen. The leader of these women, Jemima Nicholas, a local cobbler-woman, is said to have captured a dozen Frenchmen single handed, armed only with a pitchfork! Her heroism is remembered in the form of a monument in the church-yard at St. Mary's, where she is buried. Within 48 hours of landing, the French had surrendered.

The heroism of the women has been painstakingly recorded in a vivid and carefully researched tapestry measuring 30 metres which superbly characterises the event. Plans are ongoing to

Opposite: Strumble Head, near Fishguard

The Last Invasion Tapestry

find a permanent home to display this extraordinary work.

Fishguard is split into two distinct parts. The busy upper part is much like any small town, with many shops, pubs and places to eat. The Lower Town is much older and very attractive, its pretty cottages clustered around the old harbour, where the River Gwaun reaches the sea. In 1971 Lower Fishguard temporarily changed its identity to the fictional town of Llareggub when this picturesque location was chosen for the film version of Dylan Thomas's famous radio play 'Under Milk Wood', and was also the location for the making of the Orson Welles classic 'Moby Dick.'

The landscape around Fishguard is truly magnificent. To the northwest is dramatic Strumble Head, where the lighthouse is linked to the cliff by a causeway. Dinas Head dominates the coast to the northeast, while inland is the beautiful wooded Gwaun Valley. The whole area is dotted with prehistoric sites.

Melin Tregwynt Woollen Mill, Abermawr, Fishguard

For more information ring 01348 891225.

Llangloffan Farmhouse Cheese Centre, near Fishguard

Take a drive to the Pembrokeshire hamlet of Llangloffan, near Fishguard and see how Leon and Joan Downey have revived the art of traditional Welsh farmhouse cheesemaking.

From humble beginnings 25 years ago the Cheese Centre now produces 15 tons of cheese a year - a far cry from the early days when their cheese was made on the Aga for their own consumption, but the Downeys enthusiasm and drive has won them international acclaim for their enterprising business, desire to boost the rural economy and not least the wonderful flavoursome handmade cheeses, all free from artificial and

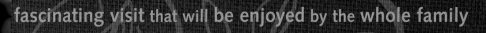
fascinating visit that will be enjoyed by the whole family

SEE THE
Cheesemaking
process...

Renowned around the world and only available from the most exclusive shops, Llangloffan Farmhouse Cheese is made in the heart of the Pembrokeshire countryside and we extend you a warm welcome to witness this fascinating process.

The cheesemaking starts at 6.00am, and when our doors open to the public at 10.00am you will be able to see the most exciting part of the process. Last admission to the demonstration is at 11.45am **– the earlier you arrive, the more you see.**

...from milk to
Llangloffan
Cheese

Goodwick
Fishguard
Tregwynt Voollen Mill
St Davids 11 miles
A487
A4219
Scleddau
A40
Mathry
Llangloffan Cheese Centre
Haverfordwest 9 miles
Castle Morris
B4331
Letterston

Cheesemaking demonstrations: begin at 10.00am and finish at 12.45pm
Easter – end September: Monday to Friday (inclusive)   **October:** Tuesday, Wednesday & Thursday
October Half-Term: Monday to Friday (inclusive)   **Open Bank Holidays**
Farm Shop: open every day 9.00am – 5.30pm (except Sundays) throughout the year.

The Gwaun Valley

*The Quay,
Lower Fishguard*

genetically modified additives, they produce.

From Easter to the end of October visitors can view the cheese-making process in the dairy daily, or visit the Tides Restaurant, run by daughter Emma which features some wonderful wholesome dishes.

For further details see our advertisements or visit www.welshcheese.co.uk

THE GWAUN VALLEY

The Gwaun Valley is exceptionally beautiful and runs inland from Lower Fishguard to its source high on the slopes of Foel Eryr in the Preseli Hills. It is one of several inland areas of Pembrokeshire which fall within the National Park, and is regarded by geologists as the best example in the British Isles, if not the world, of a sub-glacial meltwater channel.

What this means is that about 200,000 years ago, towards the end of one of several recurring Ice Ages which have gripped the planet, the climate became progressively warmer and water began to tunnel beneath the melting ice. This meltwater was under intense pressure, the ice acting as a sort of geological pipe, and it moved with such tremendous force that it flowed uphill for long stretches. As this unstoppable water eventually crashed down towards the sea, taking

with it huge boulders and blocks of ice, it created deep steep-sided gorges in the landscape. Such are the awesome forces of nature which have given us the spectacular Gwaun Valley.

The valley is narrow and sheltered, with heavily wooded sides stretching up to 200 feet high. It is rich in wildlife and prehistoric remains, with an abundance of wild flowers and such birds as the buzzard, kestrel, owl, kingfisher, warbler and dipper. The River Gwaun, low and gentle in the summer, becomes a roaring torrent in winter as it rushes down from the Preseli Hills rising behind the valley.

Most of the valley's small communities are centred around the hamlets of Llanychaer and Pontfaen. These are largely farming communities, as much of the valley floor is farmed, and several farmhouses boast interesting architectural features such as distinctive Flemish-style chimneys.

The people of the valley are distinctive too; not in appearance, but in the fact that they are sticklers for local tradition. They still celebrate New Year's Day on 13th January according to the old Gregorian calendar - despite the fact that the change to the Julian calendar was made legal in 1752!

Other interesting stones

can be seen at the restored church in picturesque Pontfaen, where memorial stones dating from the 9th century stand in the church-yard.

The ancient woodland of the Gwaun Valley is very precious, and parts of it have been designated as SSSI's - Sites of Special Scientific Interest. The species to be found here include oak, ash, sycamore, alder, blackthorn, hazel, hornbeam, wild cherry and wych elm, and the National Park Authority has established the Cilrhedyn Woodland Centre to promote good woodland management in the valley. Though very much a working centre for the Park Authority's woodland experts and rangers, it is planned to encourage visitors to the centre on a limited number of special open days during the main holiday season. More details of this can be obtained from any National Park Information Centre.

The National Park Authority has also made the valley more accessible on foot by creating the Golden Road Path. This takes you from Lower Fishguard to Crymych via the ridge of the Preseli Hills, passing such fasci-nating features as Bronze Age burial mounds, a Neolithic burial chamber, a particularly fine example of an Iron Age fort, and Carn Meini - the source of the bluestone which thousands of years ago

Newport

mysteriously found its way to Stonehenge for the construction of the monument's inner circle.

NEWPORT

Newport is a very popular resort. The charming little town sits on the lower slopes of Carn Ingli, which rises to more than 1100 feet above sea level, and the superb stretch of sands on the east side of the Nevern estuary is rivalled only by Whitesands Bay as the best beach in North Pembrokeshire.

On the opposite shore of the estuary mouth is Parrog. It was here that Newport developed as a thriving port engaged in fishing, coastal trading and shipbuilding. Herrings were exported to Ireland, France and Spain, and by 1566 Newport was an important wool centre. However, this industry faltered when an outbreak of plague hit the town during the reign of Elizabeth I and much business was lost to Fishguard. Later in the port's development, slates quarried from local cliffs went by sea to Haverfordwest, Pembroke, Tenby and parts of Ireland. In 1825 maritime trade received a boost when the quay was built, and come the end of the 19th century Newport boasted

five warehouses, several limekilns, coal yards and a shipyard. Today the estuary is silted up and pleasure craft occupy the moorings.

As for the town itself, one of the main features is Newport Castle. This overlooks the estuary and was built in the early 13th century by William FitzMartin. It has had an eventful history: captured by Llywelyn the Great in 1215, then by Llywelyn the Last in 1257, and attacked and damaged in Owain Glyndwr's revolt in 1408, after which it fell into decline. It remained a ruin until 1859, when the gatehouse and one of its towers were converted into a residence. Today the castle is in private ownership and not open to visitors. You can, however, see William FitzMartin's other contribution to Newport. He established St. Mary's, a huge church which is cruciform in plan and features a 13th-century Norman tower.

Other attractions in Newport include a 9-hole golf course alongside the sands, and the prehistoric cromlech known as Carreg Goetan Arthur, which stands in a field by the bridge. There are many such sites in the area. On Carn Ingli Common there are prehistoric hut circles and stones, and the most striking and famous site of all is Pentre Ifan, 3 miles southeast of Newport. This Neolithic

chambered tomb is one of the finest in Britain, with 3 upright stones over 6 feet high supporting a huge capstone.

DINAS CROSS

Dinas Cross and its surrounding area is notable for its prehistoric monuments, especially the Bronze Age cairns. Cairns and barrows - mounds of stone or stone and earth - were built throughout the Bronze Age (2000 - 600BC) and often mark the sites of burials. Stone cists at the centre of the mound often contain cremations and pottery vessels and it is thought that the cairns themselves acted as memorial sites.

There are at least two Bronze Age ring cairns up on Dinas Mountain, and a prehistoric standing stone just outside the village of Dinas Cross. Dinas Mountain is on the edge of the Preseli Hills, which are famous for their prehistoric monuments.

The stones for the first stone phase of Stonehenge came from Carn Meini, high in the Preselis. The whole area is littered with prehistoric sites, including Iron Age hillforts (600BC - 43AD) and earlier cairns and standing stones.

Sites like the spectacular hillfort at the summit of Carningli were clearly used over a long period of time and must have been important

Nevern Church

spiritual or religious places.

Mynydd Melyn, a short distance southeast of Dinas Mountain, contains abundant evidence of prehistoric activity including hut circles (the foundations of prehistoric dwellings) parts of a field system, and several cairns.

The West Wales ECO Centre, Newport

For more information ring 01239 820235.

NEVERN

Nevern is an ancient parish on the River Nyfer, close to Newport. Its imposing

Norman church, dedicated to the Celtic saint Brynach, has a definite mystique and atmosphere that is compounded by the famous bleeding yew in the churchyard - a broken branch that constantly drips blood-red sap. The church features a magnificent 11th-century wheel-headed Celtic cross which stands 13 feet high and rivals the cross at Carew. Above the church, topping a deep ravine, is Nevern Castle - a motte and bailey earthwork.

MOYLEGROVE

This attractive coastal village stands on the Newport-

St. Dogmael's road, a mile from Ceibwr Bay. It dates back to Norman times and nearby are two burial chambers. Small cargo ships once used the bay, and high cliffs and secluded coves mark the coast here, where Atlantic grey seals often bask.

ST. DOGMAELS

Facing Cardigan across the Teifi estuary is the picturesque hillside village of St. Dogmael's. It lies close to Poppit Sands, the most northerly beach in the National Park and also the northern end of the Pembrokeshire Coastal Path.

In St. Dogmael's you will find the remains of a 12th-century abbey built in 1115 by Benedictine monks from France - as a replacement for an earlier Celtic monastery which had stood on the site until Viking raiders destroyed it in the 10th century. The north and west walls of the nave are still standing. Next to the abbey ruins is the parish church of St. Thomas the Martyr. It contains the Sagranus Stone, which bears an inscription that proved to be the key in deciphering the ancient Ogham script in 1848.

CILGERRAN

Famous for its superb Norman castle, which is perched above the wooded gorge of the Teifi, Cilgerran is a few miles east of Cardigan and was once a slate quarrymen's village. It is the venue for the annual coracle regatta, which takes place in August.

THE TEIFI ESTUARY

The River Teifi is a natural boundary between Pembrokeshire and Ceredigion, and its wide estuary is of great interest. The large and popular beach of Poppit Sands is backed by extensive dunes and has good visitor facilities. The area is also excellent walking and watersports country, and the estuary is a favourite haunt for birdwatchers. The many species to be observed here include gulls, oystercatchers, curlews, cormorants and shelduck. The Teifi is also well known for its salmon and sea trout, and the ancient Teifi coracle was used by fishermen long before the Romans arrived.

The valley of the Teifi, which a little further inland separates the counties of Ceredigion and Carmarthenshire, is said to be one of the most beautiful river valleys in Britain. It is certainly very scenic, with several picturesque towns and villages along its banks, and for visitors to North Pembrokeshire is well worth exploring.

St. Dogmaels Abbey

Cilgerran

INLAND PEMROKESHIRE

THE PRESELI HILLS

In the ancient Welsh tales of The Mabinogion, Pembrokeshire was described as "Gwlad hud a lledrith" - the land of magic and enchantment. And nowhere is this magic and enchantment more evident than in the wild, mysterious Preseli Hills.

These rolling moorlands, often overlooked by visitors on their way to the coast, are the major upland region of the National Park, presenting a stark contrast to the relatively flat coastal plateau. The hills do not aspire to any great height - the highest summit, Foel Cwm Cerwyn, is 1760 feet above sea level - but the many remains of hillforts, burial chambers and other monuments are proof that even prehistoric man had a powerful affinity with this bleak and mystical landscape.

The evidence left by the earliest settlers suggests man has occupied the hills for at least 5000 years. Neolithic burial chambers, Bronze Age cairns, stone circles, standing stones and Iron Age forts litter this untouched Celtic landscape.

When Neolithic (New Stone Age) farmers arrived in Pembrokeshire, well versed in the art of raising crops and herding animals, they were the first people to work the land here. They fashioned implements such as axes, hammers and hoes from Preseli dolerite (bluestone), and archaeologists believe that two so-called 'axe factories' existed on the Preseli Hills, though their sites have never been identified.

The dwellings of these distant ancestors were too flimsy to stand up to the ravages of time. But not so their tombs (cromlechau), which are concentrated along the coastal

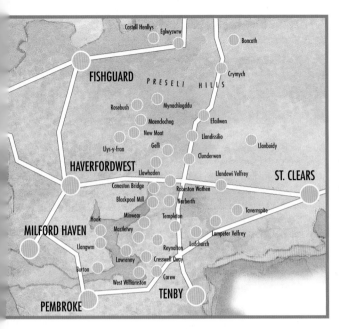

Pentre Ifan

Opposite: The Preseli Hills

plateau and in the Preseli foothills. Pentre Ifan, on the hills' northern slopes, and Carreg Samson, on the coast near Abercastle, are two of the finest prehistoric monuments to be found anywhere in Wales.

Later Bronze Age man also left his burial sites on the Preseli Hills, in the form of round cairns. A fine example is that to be found on top of Foel Drygarn. There is another on the summit of Foel Cwm Cerwyn, the highest point in all Pembrokeshire. On exceptionally clear days the views from here are astonishing. You can see west to the Wicklow Mountains of Ireland, north to Snowdonia, east to the Brecon Beacons and south across the Bristol Channel to the counties of the West Country.

Another ancient relic adorning the Preseli Hills is the interesting stone circle known as Gors Fawr. This stands on the moorland west of the hamlet of Mynachlogddu. It comprises 16 stones and 2 large outlying pointer stones, and its diameter exceeds 70 feet.

But the biggest mystery of all to emanate from these brooding hills - and one which seems unlikely ever to be answered - concerns the inner circle at Stonehenge, 180 miles from Preseli on Salisbury Plain. Much of this inner circle is made from bluestone, which is dolerite, rhyolite and volcanic ash, found only at Carn Meini on the eastern crests of the Preseli Hills. The mystery is how the 80 stones, weighing up to 4 tons each and over 250 tons in total, made the incredible journey from Preseli to

PRESELI BLUESTONE

Bluestones from the Preseli Hills make up the inner circle at Stonehenge, but how they got there is one of life's mysteries. Two theories exist as to how the stones, each weighing four tons and over 250 tons altogether made the 180-mile journey. One is that a great glacier carried them; while another more fanciful suggestion is that the builders of Stonehenge had mystical powers and used levitation to move the massive stones. A more likely explanation, however, is that they were taken by boat along rivers and up the Bristol Channel before being dragged on sledges to their final resting place.

Salisbury Plain during the third millennium BC.

The most likely explanation seems to be that they were taken by boat along rivers and up the Bristol Channel, crossing the overland stretches on sledges which had rollers underneath. This would have taken a gargantuan effort by a huge army of labour. Even so, this theory has found much wider acceptance than the two others proposed.

One is that the stones were carried to Salisbury Plain by the great Irish Sea Glacier - the biggest flow of glacial ice ever to cover Britain - long before the builders of Stonehenge set about their task. But even many geologists doubt that this is the case.

The other suggestion, and by far the most fanciful, is that levitation is the answer. It is proposed that the builders of Stonehenge had mystical powers and could magically raise stones off the ground merely by thinking about it. Other stories from around the world tell of stones being moved in this way.

The Preseli Hills have inspired other myths and legends. Predictably, King Arthur has strong associations here. A tale from The Mabinogion tells how he pursued a great black boar across these hills from Ireland, and his name is remembered in such places as Carn Arthur.

Exploring the Preseli Hills

won't bring you into contact with the legendary black boar but there are certainly other creatures of interest to see. Wild ponies still roam free on the hills, and among the birds which frequent this upland territory are kestrels, meadow pippits, skylarks and wheatears. Close to the resort town of Newport are such delights as Nevern, with its haunting church, and the reconstructed Iron Age hillfort at Castell Henllys. A little further north are the dramatic cliffs of Cemaes Head, where the exposed rocks have been folded by the tremendous forces exerted by movements deep in the earth. The cliffs of the headland are over 500 feet high in places - the highest in Pembrokeshire - and they look down to the mouth of the Teifi estuary.

Like any upland area, the Preseli Hills are best explored on foot, and apart from sheep the most common species you are likely to encounter in these wilds are hill walkers. Ornithologists, botanists, archaeologists, artists, photographers and others of strange pursuits also seem to find the hills a suitable habitat. However, unless you are familiar with the hills, it is advisable to take a map and compass on your travels. The average rainfall on the hills is nearly twice as much as it is on the coast, and the mists have a tendency to come down very suddenly.

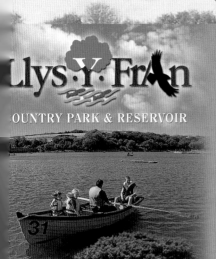

Llys·y·Frân

COUNTRY PARK & RESERVOIR

LOOK OUT FOR OUR BROCHURE

A visit to Llys-y-Frân Country Park and Reservoir has long been one of Pembrokeshire's favourite days out.

There's such a wide variety to interest the whole family – from a short stroll to a full-stretch walk, from cycling to rowing, or simply enjoying the spectacular views of the 100ft high dam and the surrounding countryside... the list is endless and we're sure you'll want to come back again and again.

For further information about Llys-y-Frân, please ring the Visitor Centre on 01437 532273 or 01437 532694 or fax us on 01437 532732.

Park open 8 am - dusk during the season (9 am in Winter)

WALKING · FISHING · CYCLING · PLAYGROUND · HIRE BOATS · RESTAURANT · GIFT SHOP

This is also the only part of Pembrokeshire where winter snow falls on anything like a regular basis.

An alternative way of exploring the Preseli Hills is to join a guided walk or horse riding session which are run throughout the year by the National Park Authority as part of its annual activities and events programme. For more information contact any National Park Information Centre.

The following is a brief survey of some of the villages and places of interest which lie on or near the slopes of the Preseli Hills and which have not been described in other parts of this guide.

Llys-y-fran Reservoir & Country Park

Close to the picturesque village of Rosebush, beautiful Llys-y-fran Country Park incorporates the 212-acre reservoir that supplies most of Pembrokeshire's drinking water. Around this man-made lake are mature woodlands and open grassland, with superb views of the Preseli Hills and surrounding farmland. In spring, the carpets of bluebells in the woods are a sheer delight, and throughout the season the country park is vibrant with the colours of countless varieties of wild flowers.

INLAND PEMBROKESHIRE

In recent years improvements have been made to the park, following a scheme to increase the size of the reservoir, an example of which is the much wider footpath right round the reservoir, and the 20,000 broad-leafed trees which have been planted. As a result, the 6½-mile perimeter walk is now even more enjoyable than ever.

Near the main car park is the children's adventure playground which is equipped to keep youngsters amused for hours. Mountain bikes are another treat families can enjoy. Bikes can be hired by the hour or by the day, and with the reservoir perimeter path serving as a cycle track, this is a fun activity in which everyone can participate.

Fishing is another leisure pursuit which has always been popular here and Llys-y-fra attracts anglers from all ove Wales and beyond. Little won der as few fisheries can matc the country park's excellen facilities. These include a pu pose-built boathouse with fleet of loch-style petro engine fishing boats - ideal fo fly fishermen.

During the season, ove 20,000 top-quality rainbov trout are released into th freedom of the lake from thei rearing cages. A healthy popu lation of brown trout adds vari ety to the sport.

For watersports enthusiasts the reservoir is perfect both fo beginners and for more experi enced sailors but you mus bring your own craft as no hire is available. The park shop does however offer launching permits for dinghies, sailboards and canoes.

Llys-y-Fran Reservoir & Country Park

As you would expect in a country park of Llys-y-fran's status and reputation, wildlife is of prime concern in the management of the park. The oak and coniferous woodlands and rough grass provide ideal habitats for a variety of birds. More than 140 species have been recorded here.

Llys-y-fran's licensed restaurant enjoys superb views across the reservoir and countryside and is housed in the Visitor Centre alongside the gift and souvenir shop. The restaurant offers excellent service and opens throughout the season.

It is also worth noting that Llys-y-fran Country Park has strong historical and musical connections. Near the base of the reservoir dam is a tumble-down cottage - the birthplace of the famous Welsh composer William 'Penfro' Rowlands. It was in gratitude for his son's recovery from a serious illness that he was inspired to write the tune for Blaenwern, one of the best loved of all hymn tunes. A monument to William Rowlands, erected by Welsh Water, now stands near the ruins of the old cottage.

For further information ring 01437 532273/532694.

ROSEBUSH

Rosebush enjoys an unusual if modest claim to fame - slates from its quarries were used to roof the Houses of Parliament. But the village could have become a well-known tourist attraction in the 19th century, had everything gone according to plan. When the Clunderwen-Maenclochog railway opened in 1876 to serve the quarry there were big ambitions to develop Rosebush as an inland spa. A small tourist industry did develop here, but nothing like on the scale imagined.

Rosebush is close to Llys-y-fran Reservoir and Country Park and stands below the summit of Foel Cwm Cerwyn, in a superb setting which is ideal for walking. In 1992 a visitor centre and museum was opened in the village's old post office.

Rosebush Reservoir

MYNACHLOGDDU

This small pastoral community of the Preseli Hills once belonged to the monastery at St. Dogmael's. It stands east of Rosebush, close to the impressive Gors Fawr Stone Circle, which is over 70 feet in diameter. A commemorative stone to the poet Waldo Williams is also nearby.

NEW MOAT

This small village stands in the Preseli foothills, just east of Llys-y-fran Country Park. A mound marks the site of a Norman motte and bailey castle. The church, distinctive for its tall tower, has an early 17th century altar tomb.

MAENCLOCHOG

A small Victorian churc on the village green is the cen tral feature of this sprawlin community on the souther slopes of the Preseli Hills, couple of miles north-east of Llys-y-fran Country Park. Fo many years the village ha served the needs of the area and early this centur Maenclochog boasted a black smith, miller, carpenter, lim burner, wheelwright, drape and no fewer than 10 pubs! A mile from the village is Penrhos - the only thatched

...ottage in the area, and now a museum.

CRYMYCH

Crymych, situated on the A478 Tenby-Cardigan road, is a 19th-century hillside village which grew up around the railway. The Whitland-Cardigan line was completed in 1880 and no longer exists, but the village has remained an important agricultural centre and is an ideal base from which to explore the Preseli Hills. Within easy reach are Foel Drygarn, where cairns and an early Iron Age fort are to be found, and the 1300-feet summit of Y Frenni Fawr.

BONCATH

Between Crymych and Newcastle Emlyn, Boncath takes it's name from the Welsh word for buzzard. A former railway village, it is notable for two houses - Ffynone, designed by John Nash in 1792, and Cilwendeg, a Georgian house built by Morgan Jones.

EGLWYSWRW

A compact little village near Castell Henllys Iron Age fort, north of the Preseli Hills, this place with the unpronounceable name (at least, to the English!) is where St. Wrw is buried. The pre-Christian churchyard is circular, and other interesting historical features include the medieval inn, the remains of a motte and bailey castle, and a prehistoric ringwork.

Castell Henllys Iron Age Fort

This remarkable and archaeologically important example of an Iron Age fort is managed by the National Park Authority and has been partially reconstructed with thatched roundhouses, animal pens, a smithy and a grain store, all standing on their original sites. More recently the site was the location of the BBC's 'Surviving the Iron Age' series.

The Visitor Centre houses an exhibition which serves as

Preseli Mountains

Rosebush

an introduction to the life of the early Celts in Wales. Castell Henllys probably flourished between the 4th century BC and 1st century AD, when the Romans began their conquest of Britain. The Iron Age Celts were a fierce and warlike people, and many of their chieftains lived in well-defended forts, of which Castell Henllys was typical. Sited on a valley spur, it had natural defences on three sides, and where the spur joined the side of the valley massive earthworks were thrown up, topped with timber palisades. Stone walling protected a narrow gateway which can still be seen. Such elaborate defences would have employed a huge labour force, and this suggests that Castell Henllys was occupied by a leader of some importance, along with family, retainers and even a band of warriors.

The introduction to the site of domestic animals which flourished in the Iron Age has given a further insight into the daily life of these ancient ancestors. A self-guided trail takes you through Castell Henllys, with informative interpretative panels along the way. This is a wonderful place for schools and study groups, and an Education Centre has been built in the valley below the fort. To further recapture the atmosphere and spirit of this mystical historic site, which stands in beautiful North Pembrokeshire coun-

tryside below the summit Carn Ingli, special events a held throughout the holid season, including shows give by the Prytani - an Iron Ag Celtic re-enactment grou Castell Henllys, just off th A486 a few miles east Newport, is open daily fro Easter to October.

For further information rin 01239 891319 or visit our websit www.castellhenllys.com

THE LANDSKER BORDERLANDS

When the Normans invade Pembroke in 1093 and too the site on which the magnifi cent castle now stands, the were quick to consolidat their domination of Sout Pembrokeshire and the land they had gained here. To th north of the county th rebellious Welsh proved mor troublesome. The Norman response was to build a line o castles to protect their newly won territory, effectively dividing north from south.

These formidable fortresse stretched from Llanstephan in the southeast to Roch in the northwest. They marked wha has become known as the Landsker Line - a word of Norse origin meaning frontier. Originally a military device, the Landsker evolved into a cultural and linguistic divide, and its effects are evident even today.

For example, in the north of the county Welsh is still spoken and many of the place names are Welsh also. Churches are usually small, with bellcotes and no towers. By comparison, in the anglicised south English is the dominant language, as is clear from the names of the towns and villages, and the Norman churches are characterised by tall, square towers which served as lookouts.

One of the castles of the Landsker Line was Narberth. Its scant ruins still stand near the centre of this important market town, which is 10 miles north of Tenby. Narberth is at the heart of a beautiful and historic part of inland Pembrokeshire known as the Landsker Borderlands. The Borderlands spill over into old Carmarthenshire and are bounded by the River Taf to the east, the Daugleddau estuary to the west, hills and valleys to the north and vales and plains to the south. As awareness of the Borderlands increases, a growing number of visitors are exploring this largely undiscovered area of great rural delights.

The attractive countryside of the Landsker Borderlands, rich in heritage and wildlife, is typified in the north by lush farmland sweeping down from

Celtic crafts at Castell Henllys

St. Andrews Church Narberth

Llawhaden Castle

the Preseli Hills. Here you will discover quiet river valleys and tranquil riverside communities, such as those of Lawrenny and Landshipping on the upper reaches of the Daugleddau estuary.

South of the Landsker, the rural landscape belies its industrial past. It is hard to believe, for example, that small villages like Reynalton and Jeffreston were once at the heart of the thriving Pembrokeshire coalfield.

Like all Pembrokeshire, the Landsker Borderlands display evidence of a long history and of occupation by very early settlers. There are prehistoric sites at Holgan Camp, Llawhaden - an Iron Age hill fort - and remains of settlements in Canaston Woods near Canaston Bridge. Medieval ruins are plentiful including the Sisters House in ancient Minwear Woods, the hospice chapel and castle-cum-bishop's palace in Llawhaden and the mighty Norman castles of Carew and Manorbier.

The Borderlands are also a natural draw for all who appreciate wildlife. During spring and summer the hedgerows and woodlands are ablaze with the colours of snowdrops, primroses, campions, cowslips, foxgloves, blue-

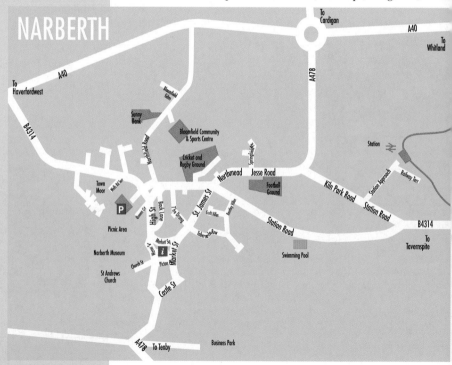

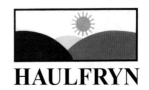

bells, dog roses, cow parsley, honeysuckle and many varieties of common and rare orchids. In autumn, fungi and ferns brighten the woodland floor, and butterflies, moths and damselflies bring dashes of colour to the air. Birds and mammals are in abundance too. Buzzards, tawny owls, grey herons, kingfishers, woodpeckers and numerous species of waders and dippers can all be seen in the Borderlands, along with foxes, badgers and even elusive otters. In spring, you might also spot the rare Tenby daffodil, which is particular to this area.

NARBERTH

Distances: Fishguard 24, Haverfordwest 9, Milford Haven 14, Pembroke 15, St. Davids 25, Tenby 10, Carmarthen 21 & London 241.

This delightful little town, with its colour-washed Georgian houses, castle ruins and amazing variety of original shops is an essential visit.

In recent years the town has become a centre for artists and craftspeople, many of whose works are sold here. Jewellery, pottery, paintings, fabrics, glassware, clothing,

Narberth

INLAND PEMBROKESHIRE

Narberth

woodworks are all represented. Some of the shops and galleries sell a variety of goods, others specialise in the makers own work. If the creativity of the place starts to inspire you, there is even a cafe where you can decorate a pot or plate yourself while enjoying your coffee and call back to fetch it after firing.

This creative movement may be relatively recent, but Narberth's history is a long and fascinating one. Standing just south of the Landsker, it falls into the area regarded as 'Little England beyond Wales' but its roots lie deep in Welsh history, culture and tradition. The Welsh princes of Dyfed

lived here in the dark ages and the town - called by its Welsh name, Arberth, features in the ancient stories of the Mabinigion. Narberth Castle of which little now remains was part of the Norman frontier separating north from south. It was captured by the Welsh on numerous occasions and destroyed by Cromwell's forces during the Civil War.

Narberth is also remembered for the infamous Rebecca Riots of the 19th century. These began in 1839 with the burning of toll gates in Efailwen, a hamlet in the Preseli foothills a few miles north of the town. This anger was in response to the decision by rich landowners to impose crippling road tolls on the small and impoverished farming communities. The men responsible for torching the toll gates avoided recognition by dressing in women's clothing and blackening their faces, and they addressed their leader as 'Rebecca'. The dispute quickly became more widespread and other toll gates were destroyed just as quickly as they could be erected. The riots, often described as a 'true people's revolt' because they had their cause in natural justice, went on for a period of several years. It is one of the ironies of local history that when the authorities called out the

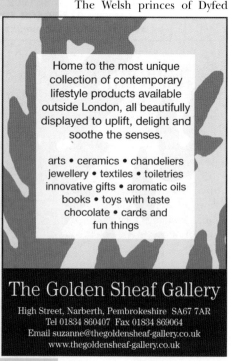

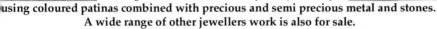
troops in a bid to discover the identity of Rebecca and his followers, they were billeted in Narberth's poorhouse.

Rebecca's Cell can be seen under the old Town Hall which now houses a craft shop.

Narberth Castle, of which little now remains, was part of the Norman frontier separating north from south. It was captured by the Welsh on numerous occasions and destroyed in the Civil War by Cromwell's forces. The castle ruins are currently under restoration and are open to visitors in the summer months.

Narberth's small but attractive town centre is distinctive for its Town Hall and pleasant Georgian houses. With the promotion of the Landsker Borderlands and other rural tourist areas, Narberth has been revitalised. PLANED (Pembrokeshire Local Action Network for Enterprise and Development) has its headquarters here, and the town is very close to a number of the county's most popular attractions. The list is impressive: Heron's Brook Leisure Park, Oakwood, Canaston Centre, Blackpool Mill, Picton Castle, Llawhaden Castle, Holgan Camp Iron Age Hillfort and Folly Farm. These are in addition to those places of interest in Narberth itself, which include the Queens Hall, Golden Sheaf Gallery, Creative Café and a wealth of interesting and unusual shops, such as Furious Fish, Haulfryn and Fabric House.

Narberth

Canaston Bridge

Creative Café

A studio/café with a difference, where *you* can be the artist - whether you're artistic or not.

Enjoy painting your own designs on ready-made pottery - egg cups, pet bowls, house signs, etc - leave it with us to glaze and fire, then collect 1-3 days later.

A delicious range of teas, special coffees, snacks and home-made cakes are available. Booking is advisable on wet days.

For more information ring 01834 861651.

Heron's Brook Leisure Park and Approach Golf Course

A countryside attraction near the centre of Narberth the park is set in 30 acres of parkland and offers a good family day out. For keen and budding golfers, there's the challenge of 9-hole pitch & putt and an 18-hole approach golf course.

For more information ring 01834 860723.

The Queen's Hall

A great arts, music and entertainment venue situated in High Street (next to the town's free car park) with a variety of events to suit all tastes. Gallery and cafe.

For more information ring the Box Office on 01834 861212.

CANASTON BRIDGE

Just west of Narberth, Canaston Bridge marks the junction of the A40 and A4075. This attractive wooded area is the northern boundary of the Eastern Cleddau, and from here you can join the Knightsway - a 9-mile walk linking the Daugleddau Trail with the coast path at Amroth. Nearby, on the south side of the A40, is a picnic area and restored Blackpool Mill, and a mile or so from the north side is the impressive ruin of Llawhaden Castle. A few miles south, on the A4075, are the

neighbouring attractions of Oakwood and Canaston Centre. Also within the area are several interesting woodland walks, including a relatively short path which takes you to Blackpool Mill.

Oakwood & CC2000

One of the top ten theme parks in the UK, Oakwood has over 40 rides and attractions for all the family, whatever the weather. Next door is CC2000, Oakwood's indoor bowling and family entertainment Centre.
For more information see Pembrokeshire's Premier Attractions section.

Blackpool Mill

In a beautiful setting on the banks of the Eastern Cleddau, this is one of the finest examples in Wales of a mill complete with all of its machinery. You can visit their Museum, gift shop and tea room which are open from Easter to September.
For more information ring 01437 541233.

CLUNDERWEN

Situated just inside Carmarthenshire and known until the 1870's as Narberth Road. The village of Clunderwen developed with the coming of the railway in 1852. An interesting historical anecdote is that it was here in 1913 that the James Brothers first flew their bi-plane - one of the earliest flights in Wales.

EFAILWEN

A small community north of Narberth, in the southern Preseli foothills, Efailwen is recorded in the history books as the place where the erection of a toll gate in 1839 sparked off the Rebecca Riots. Nearby, at Glandy Cross, is a group of Neolithic and Bronze Age sites, regarded as the most important in South Wales.

GELLI

Located just north of Llawhaden, the small community of Gelli developed around a large woollen mill. This worked from the late 19th century until 1937, and was one of several mills which flourished in the Landsker Borderlands at that time. Fishing was another important industry here. In the late 19th century 6 pairs of Cleddau coracles fished between Gelli and Llawhaden.

LAMPETER VELFREY

It is thought that the Landsker Line, were it ever drawn, would pass through the parish of Lampeter Velfrey, which is a few miles due east of Narberth. There are several prehistoric sites in the

Blackpool Mill

Gelli

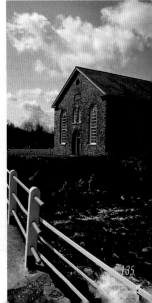

135

immediate area, including tumuli, a Bronze Age hearth and 3 Neolithic burial chambers.

are made at the Welsh Chocolate Farm at Llanboidy.
For further information ring 01994 448800.

LLANBOIDY

Llanboidy lies across the border in old Carmarthenshire, about 5 miles north of Whitland, in the small Gronw Valley. A well in the village was the focus of many medieval pilgrimages, and close to Llanboidy are two ancient sites - a cromlech at Cefn Brafle and Arthur's Table, a tumulus, which is in a wood at Dolwilym. Today the village enjoys fame as the home of Pemberton's Victorian Chocolates. See how their chocolates

LLANDDEWI VELFREY

Located between Narberth and Whitland on the busy A40, Llanddewi Velfrey originally grew around its ancient church, and there is evidence of occupation during the Iron Age.

The Quaker burial ground also reflects a strong tradition of non-conformity. The area around the village is ideal for country walks, with stunning views of the Marlais Valley to the south and the Preseli Hills to the north.

Llawhaden

LLANDISSILIO

This village stands on the A478 north of Narberth, a road which has developed from a prehistoric route that linked the Preseli Hills and the Cleddau estuary. Castle sites and earthworks suggest that the parish has a long history - an idea supported by the inscribed stones in the church which date from the 5th or 6th century.

LLANGOLMAN

From Efailwen, on the A478, the road to Llangolman gives breathtaking views of the approaching Preseli Hills.

Until a few years ago, this small village encompassed the last working Pembrokeshire slate quarry - Gilfach. The slate, which was formed from volcanic ash and is a lovely soft green colour, was highly prized, and was used to roof the National Library of Wales in Aberystwyth and to line the Suez Canal.

The Slate Workshop, on the outskirts of the village, still uses some of the green Pembrokeshire slate, although the majority now comes from other Welsh quarries.

LLAWHADEN

Llawhaden was an important medieval settlement standing on the Landsker Line, and the original Norman castle was later developed as a magnificent bishop's palace by the Bishops of St. Davids. The ruins which stand today are evidence of the grandeur of this fortified palatial residence. You can also see the remains of a medieval hospice chapel. The Norman church of St. Aidan stands in the valley below, on the banks of the Eastern Cleddau, in a very picturesque position.

Llawhaden Castle

Originally a wooden structure built in Norman times, the castle was rebuilt by the Bishops of St. Davids

Llawhaden Castle

INLAND PEMBROKESHIRE

between the late 13th and 15th centuries and transformed into a great-fortified palace. This comprised several buildings set around a five-sided courtyard, strengthened with angled corners. The ruins, now in the care of Cadw (Welsh Historic Monuments), include the front of the gatehouse, which still stands to its full height, the Great Hall, bakehouse, barracks, visitors' lodgings and the Chapel of the Blessed Virgin. After using the castle for more than 250 years, the bishops dismantled it and stripped the lead from the roof. Close to the castle are two other historic attractions - a restored medieval hospice and Holgan Camp, an Iron Age fort to which visitors now have access thanks to the opening of a new public footpath. The site of the camp was overgrown for centuries until cleared and fenced by PLANED - the Pembrokeshire Local Action Network for Enterprise and Development - and Cadw. Holgan Camp had formidable defences, and is a well-preserved example of an Iron Age defended enclosure. Many such camps were established in this area.

Sycamores Ranch
Western Riding Centre
Llawhaden, Narberth,
Pembrokeshire
Tel: 01437 541298
(For more information see our advert on page 177)

LUDCHURCH

Located less than 3 mile south-east of Narberth Ludchurch stands on the route of the Knightsway footpath. A curious fact is that prior to the 1950's, the name Ludchurch referred only to the Norman church and parish, and the village itself was known as Egypt! There are definitely no pyramids here but there are some fine lime kilns to be seen in the old quarry, which today is a beautifully landscaped area. The name Ludchurch is also becoming increasingly well known among people with good taste. The reason is Princes Gate Water - spring water of exceptionally pure quality which has proven so popular that it is now supplied all over Wales and to markets as far apart as London and North America. The water comes from 3 acres of farmland in the parish which are saturated with clean natural springs.

REYNALTON

Reynalton, situated west of Begelly and south of Narberth, is now a small, quiet hamlet in the midst of farmland. Yet earlier in the century coal mining was a thriving local industry, as the village stands in the old South Pembrokeshire coalfield.

LITTLE KINGS
PARK

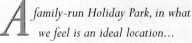

A family-run Holiday Park, in what we feel is an ideal location...

Set in a quiet country lane, Little Kings is just 1½ miles from the beach at Amroth and the stunning views from the park span the whole of Carmarthen Bay — from Monkstone Point to the Gower Peninsula and beyond to the Somerset and North Devon coastline, Caldey and Lundy Islands.

We can offer you luxury holiday accommodation in one of our caravan holiday homes, and we also welcome tourers, motorhomes and tents.

We look forward to welcoming you to our Park — we love it here and hope that you will too.

Little Kings Park
Ludchurch, Amroth, Pembrokeshire SA67 8PG
www.littlekings.co.uk

Call 01834 831330
for a FREE brochure

*Church of The
Holy Cross,
Robeston Wathen*

ROBESTON WATHEN

The earliest record of Robeston Wathen dates back as far as 1282. The small hilltop community, on the A40, has a Norman church and its distinctive tower.

The part of the parish name Robeston is of Norman origin, whose Kings sought to impose their rule on this part of Wales. The Parish was celled at this time Villa Robti or "Robert's Ton", although no records indicate who Robert was. However in the 13th century a family by the name of Wathen was granted the titular Lordship of the Manor, and so the village has been named Robeston Wathen ever since.

This family had interests in the production and weaving of wool, which was to remain the major export of England and Wales for several centuries. Some indication of the importance of this trade can be seen from the fact that Geoffrey Chaucer, the author of Canterbury tales earned his living as the King's Wool Talleyman. Today, he would be called a Chief Inspector of Customs and Excise.

The Wathen family moved to the Cotswolds, Gloucester and Bristol in Elizabethan times – then great centres of the wool trade. The Wathen family have served with distinction in Church, State and banking. One John d Wathen became Bishop o Salisbury, and his 14th centur tomb can be seen in Westminster Abbey.

TAVERNSPITE

Tavernspite is on the Pembrokeshire Carmarthen shire border at the junction o the B4328 and B4314. At on time this was also on the rout of the mail coaches which travelled from London t Ireland via Milford Haven The local community her takes great pride in the village in recent years Tavernspite ha won awards in competition for Wales In Bloom and Bes Kept Village. Tavernspite i also notable for its chapel - one of the most remote and picturesque in Pembroke shire.

TEMPLETON

The layout of Templeton, which is a mile south of Narberth, is a fine example of village planning in the Middle Ages. It is believed that the Knights Templars had a hospice here - possibly on the site now occupied by St. John's church - and in the 13th century the village was known as the settlement of the Templars. Hence the name Templeton today. There are several ancient sites here, including Sentence Castle, originally a raised fortification which also probably dates from the time of the Knights Templars. The Knightsway trail passes through the village.

WISTON

The village of Wiston, five miles north-east of Haverfordwest, was an important settlement in medieval times. Wiston Castle was at a strategic point on the Landsker line and as such was the scene of much bloodshed in the 12th and 13th centuries. The remains of this impressive stone motte and bailey castle are a short walk from the car park in the centre of the village and now administered by CADW. Admission is free.

THE DAUGLEDDAU

The Daugleddau estuary is an area of great natural beauty, comprising the fascinating stretch of waterway which extends inland from the Haven and encompasses four rivers - Western Cleddau, Eastern Cleddau, Carew and Cresswell. It is an inner sanctuary, often described as the hidden treasure of the Pembrokeshire Coast National Park. Daugleddau (which means two rivers of the Cleddau) begins east of the Cleddau toll bridge, and has become known as The Secret Waterway.

In recognition of the Daugleddau's remarkable diversity of flora and fauna, many parts of the waterway are designated Sites of Special Scientific Interest. These include the Carew and Cresswell rivers, Lawrenny Wood, Minwear Wood, parts of Slebech Park, and West Williamston Quarries.

In Tudor times Lawrenny was famous for its oysters. By the 19th century sailing vessels of all shapes and sizes - brigantines, ketches, sloops, schooners and coasters - were busily importing and exporting coal, grain, limestone, timber and general goods.

Towards the latter part of the century, Willy Boys - flat, barge-like craft - carried local produce and ran a shuttle service between seagoing vessels and the Daugleddau's upper reaches.

The poor acidic soils of West Wales made lime a valuable and highly saleable commodity. Limestone was quarried at West Williamston, Garron Pill and Llangwm Ferry and burned in hundreds of kilns along the waterway and coastline, from South Pembrokeshire to Cardigan Bay. The remains of several kilns are still visible.

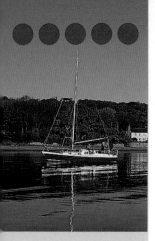

INLAND PEMBROKESHIRE

The band of carboniferous coal measures which runs across Pembrokeshire from St. Bride's Bay to Saundersfoot cuts through the uppermost reaches of the Daugleddau, and mining around Landshipping was at its height in the first half of the 19th century - particularly after the introduction in 1800 of the first steam engine to be used in a Pembrokeshire coalfield. The high-quality anthracite was in great demand. But a tragic accident at the Garden Pit near Landshipping in 1844, and a series of insurmountable geological problems which plagued the coalfield throughout its working life, led to a rapid decline of the industry by the early 20th century. The last colliery to work, at Hook on the Western Cleddau, was closed by the National Coal Board in 1949.

The waterway's rich oak woodlands helped encourage boatbuilding, and cutters, smacks and schooners were built at yards and quays along the Daugleddau. At Lawrenny alone, over 40 sailing vessels were built during the first half of the 19th century.

Other industries flourished too - from a chemical works at Whalecomb to a furnace and forge which operated on the site now occupied by Blackpool Mill.

During the 19th century over 100 men earned their living by compass net fishing a traditional method, suited to rivers with fast-flowing tidal currents, which required considerable skill and courage.

Much of the working life of the Daugleddau centred around Lawrenny Quay, which in its heyday had more than one quay. Today it is noted for its Yacht Station and excellent facilities for pleasure craft and seeing the waterway from the comfort of a boat will take you to places inaccessible by any other means.

But whatever your method of exploration, the Daugleddau will provide endless relaxation and enjoyment.

Sights worth seeking out are many and varied, and include Lawrenny village and its well-restored cottages and huge Norman church. A National Park picnic site gives superb views over the Carew and Cresswell rivers.

At Cresswell Quay, a picnic site and pub are just yards from the water's edge, where kingfishers and herons feed in full view.

The long-distance Daugleddau Trail and other footpaths reveal a succession of delights, from the evocative ruins of magnificent Carew Castle to the ancient woodland of Minwear.

And there are many other historic sites to enjoy, such as the exotic gardens of Upton Castle and Picton Castle and the restored mills at Carew and Blackpool.

The limestone quarries have long since fallen silent, but today West Williamston is the centre of other important work for the waterway - the rescue, nursing and rehabilitation of injured and contaminated seabirds, at the Oiled Bird Rescue Centre. Regular visitors to the centre each year are substantial numbers of Manx shearwaters, which once blown inland by autumn gales are unable to take off again and are often stranded in brightly-lit harbours and resorts such as Tenby.

BURTON

Sitting just across the Cleddau toll bridge from Pembroke Dock, and close to Neyland, Burton is a small hillside village which enjoys superb views over the waterway. It is best known as a boating centre and for its popular waterfront pub, which as well as good food boasts a large beer garden and panoramic views over the estuary to the south, east and west.

CAREW

The most southerly point of the Daugleddau section of the National Park, Carew is famous for its magnificent riverside castle, fine Celtic cross and restored tidal mill. There is also a picnic site and car park here, accessible from the village across the old narrow bridge. The village itself is small, neat and has a distinct charm, with a pub and a restaurant offering plenty of local hospitality. Close to Carew, on the south side of the

Carew Castle

143

Carew Castle

A477, is the slumbering hamlet of Carew Cheriton. The church here dates from the late 14th century and is distinctive for its very tall tower, which has a corner steeple. In the churchyard there is a detached mortuary chapel.

Carew Castle

Here is a castle which has everything: magnificent ruins, an evocative setting, a long and important history, examples of medieval and Elizabethan architecture, a Celtic cross which is one of the finest in Wales, archaeological deposits dating back over the last 2000 years - and (what castle is complete without them?) two ghosts!

Carew is undoubtedly a king among castles. It stands on a low limestone ridge at the head of a tidal inlet of the Carew River - a strategic position, as it guarded a crossing of the river and the main road to Pembroke, 5 miles away. In times of war it could also be supplied by boat, as it had access to the open sea via the Daugleddau and the Haven waterway.

Carew Castle was occupied continuously from the 12th century to the end of the 17th century, during which time it was gradually transformed from a medieval fortress to an Elizabethan mansion of con-siderable splendour. Most photographs today tend to emphasise the latter, as the castle is often shot from across the water of Carew Pill to capture one of the ruin's most striking features - the great Renaissance north wing which Sir John Perrot began building in 1588. Perrot died in 1592 of natural causes while imprisoned in the Tower of London, and the wing was never completed.

In April 1507 the castle and nearby Carew Meadows were the site of the Great Tournament - a spectacular 5-day event, attended by over 600 noblemen. The occasion was in honour of the Tudor monarchy and also to celebrate the fact that Henry VII had bestowed upon Sir Rhys ap Thomas, who held the castle at that time, the Order of the Knight of the Garter. (Sir Rhys had played a major part in Henry's victory at Bosworth and was knighted on the battlefield; it is even said that Richard III died at his hands). Although the king himself was not in attendance, the tournament was a grand affair on a scale not previously seen in Wales. The huge assembly enjoyed jousting, sword displays, hunting and other sports of the day, and the Great Hall was the scene of a sumptuous banquet. This was the last event of its kind ever staged in Britain.

During the Civil War years of 1644 and 1645, the castle changed hands between royalist and parliamentarian forces no fewer than four times. Towards the end of the century, it was abandoned by the Carew family and fell into decline.

The history of any castle which enjoyed such a long period of occupancy is obviously complex, involving many families, characters and events. But the exciting thing about Carew Castle is that much is still being discovered about its very early history. Since 1986 it has been the subject of a phased but intensive archaeological sur-vey involving excavation, a stone-by-stone study of the surviving walls and buildings, and exami-nation of doc-uments. To date, two major surprises have been unearthed. One is that the Norman part of the castle is much bigger and older than previously suspected. The other is the discovery of pre-Norman fortifications, adding weight to speculation that the site had a royal significance long before the Normans arrived and was the seat of Welsh kings throughout the Roman and Dark Age periods. This idea is supported by the famous Carew Cross, which stands within the Castle Field and is a memorial to a Welsh king who died in 1035 - more than half a century before the Normans took Pembroke in 1093.

In the near future visitors to the castle will be able to see some of the discoveries made by the archaeological survey, as there are plans to build an Interpretation Centre on site. The castle is still privately owned by descendants of the Carew family, but is leased to the Pembrokeshire Coast National Park Authority under a 99-year agreement so that the castle and its surrounding earthworks can be conserved for everyone's enjoyment. Carew is the only castle managed by the National Park Authority.

For more information ring 01646 651782.

Carew Cross

Carew's famous 11th-century Celtic Cross stands close to the castle. It is a royal memorial commemorating Maredudd ap Edwin, who in 1033 became joint ruler with his brother of Deheubarth, the kingdom of southwest Wales. Just two years later he was killed in battle. The cross comprises two separate pieces and the inscriptions are pre-dominantly Celtic but also reflect Scandinavian inf-luence.

For more information ring 01646 651782.

Carew Cross

Carew Tidal Mill

This is the only tidal mill to remain intact in Wales, and it stands on the causeway which dams the 23-acre millpond. The present mill is 19th century but the site was previously occupied by a medieval building which operated in Elizabethan times. The mill's machinery was powered by water stored at flood tide and released through sluices to drive two undershot mill wheels. It continued to grind corn commercially until 1937 and was restored in 1972. Today it is often known as the French mill - a reference to either the architectural style of the building or the mill's grinding stones, which were imported from France. As with Carew Castle, the mill is managed by the National Park Authority. It is open to visitors throughout the summer and is a popular and fascinating attraction.

For more information ring 01646 651657.

Upton Castle Grounds

Upton Castle grounds and gardens occupy a secluded wooded valley which runs down to a tributary of the Carew River. Since 1976 they have been managed and maintained by the Pembrokeshire Coast National Park Authority, and there is free parking on site. The grounds contain over 250 different species of trees and shrubs.

For more information contact any National Park Information Centre.

CRESSWELL QUAY

This is a beautiful spot for a picnic, or to enjoy a pint or Sunday lunch at the old riverside pub. The tidal Cresswell River attracts herons and a variety of other waders, and brilliantly coloured kingfishers often catch the eye as they dive for prey and seek out the best perches along the banks. Across the water, high above the steep wooded slopes, buzzards soar effortlessly over the trees of Scotland Wood.

HOOK

There is much evidence here of the area's long and intensive coalmining activities, including the remains of two quays, tramways, and bell-shaped mines from the 17th and 18th centuries. Hook Pit did not close until 1949, and in its later days was linked to the Milford Haven railway. It is a small settlement on the eastern banks of the Daugleddau, near the confluence of the Western and Eastern Cleddau rivers. Across the river, close to Picton Point, is the site from which the Picton Ferry once operated.

Coal was a valuable commodity here as the mining industry thrived for a period in the 19th century, and Landshipping Quay exported coal from several pits. Close by is the site of the terrible Garden Pit colliery disaster of 1844, when high tide flooded the mine and 40 lives were lost, including those of several young boys.

LAWRENNY

Lawrenny has an impressive church with a large Norman tower. Using the site once occupied by Lawrenny Castle - an 18th-century mansion now demolished - the National Park Authority has established a picnic area, with superb views over the Daugleddau. Earlier last century, at Lawrenny Home Farm, Mr. J.F. Lort-Phillips trained racehorses and put the village on the map when Kirkland won the Grand National in 1905. Another horseracing connection , nearby Coedcanlas was the birthplace of famous jockey turned best-selling author Dick Francis.

Lawrenny Quay

Close to Lawrenny village, Lawrenny Quay is a popular area for boating which once

Magnificent views of the Estuary - seen from Quayside Tea Rooms

QUAYSIDE
LAWRENNY
Magnificent Waterside Views

Homemade Cakes ◆ Clotted Cream Teas ◆ Local Crab & Lobster ◆ Freshly Baked Baguettes ◆ Take Away Freshly Ground Coffees ◆ Chandlery ◆ Cards & Gifts Pickles & Preserves ◆ Circular Walks

Pembrokeshire at its best
Open daily 10.30 - 5pm Easter to September
Lawrenny Quay 01646 651574
Lawrenny signposted from Carew & Oakwood

Quayside Tearoom at Lawrenny Quay is in a unique position with amazing waterside views. It is nestled in the heart of the Pembrokeshire National Park, situated on the Daugleddau estuary, often described as 'The Secret Waterway'. The tearoom has undergone complete refurbishment; character chapel chairs and pine floorboards, blended with a mix of fresh sympathetic colours, make the tearoom a calm and tranquil place to sit and relax. Outside there is a large low walled terrace giving magnificent views of the waterway, where you can sit and enjoy the great natural beauty of the estuary; waterfowl, seals, yachts and boats, all ebb and flow with the river.

At the Quayside Tearoom food is freshly prepared using as much Pembrokeshire produce as possible. Homemade cakes, bread freshly baked on the premises, along with daily specials such as locally caught crab, Pembrokeshire Cheese & Ham Platter and our special Quayside Clotted Cream Tea, freshly ground coffees, speciality teas and Italian ice cream. Gifts are also available such as handmade cards, framed artwork, local honey, pickles and preserves.

At the Quayside Tearoom you will find a warm and friendly service, with attention to detail in beautiful surroundings.

A visit to Lawrenny Quayside Tearoom is definitely worth putting on your places to visit list, to experience Pembrokeshire at its best.

Lawrenny Church

INLAND PEMBROKESHIRE

boasted a thriving shipbuilding industry. During the Second World War, Lawrenny Quay served as a marine air base for 764 Squadron of the Fleet Air Arm. Up to 15 Walrus seaplanes could be seen moored on the river, and the officers were billeted at Lawrenny Castle.

LLANGWM

Llangwm has a long history, and is said to have been a Flemish settlement in the Middle Ages. Traditionally, the main occupations of the villagers were oyster and herring fishing, with mining rising in importance in the 19th century. Llangwm is well known for its reputedly tough breed of fisherwomen, who until this century were a familiar sight on Pembrokeshire roads, carrying baskets of fish on their heads to sell in the towns. Near to Llangwm is Black Tar, a popular spot for boating and watersports enthusiasts.

MARTLETWY

A small agricultural community east of Landshipping, Martletwy is now the unlikely home of a vineyard - Cwm Deri - the only commercial vineyard in Pembrokeshire. Another product associated with Martletwy is coal, though this industry has long since vanished. Among the interesting historic buildings here is the church.

MINWEAR

A large area of the precious and ancient Minwear Wood is a designated SSSI - Site of Special Scientific Interest - and in the heart of the wood is the 12th-century church. Close by are the ruins of the medieval Sisters Houses, which once accommodated pilgrims bound for the monastic community at St. Davids. Minwear Wood is close to Blackpool Mill and Canaston Bridge.

WEST WILLIAMSTON

When the limestone quarries were established here, this medieval farming hamlet was transformed into a busy quarrymen's village with smithies, inns and its own church. Today the area has reverted to farming, and is also the home of the important Oiled Bird Rescue Centre.

The Oiled Bird Rescue Centre

A vital local resource because of the proximity of refineries and supertankers in the Milford Haven waterway. The Centre is funded entirely by voluntary contributions and welcomes visitors, but it's advisable to ring beforehand.

For more information ring 01646 651236.

Greenways Holidays

Greenways Holidays offers the best possible introduction to the natural landscape of Pembrokeshire through a wide selection of packaged and tailor-made holidays. Our comfortable farm and county guesthouse accommodations provide a warm and genuine welcome, and the perfect base from which to explore, discover, relax and be inspired by our beautiful countryside.

Whatever your interest - distance walking, leisurely back-roads cycling, or drifting along and soaking up the local heritage and culture - we offer a care-free open door to the countryside. Choose from our standard itineraries, or let us tailor-make one just for you. Our tours include booking of graded accommodation, station and luggage transfers, cycle and safety equipment hire, itinerary and maps. We take care of the details, leaving you free to enjoy the natural landscape of Pembrokeshire, the "green" way.

For further information, call 01834 862109, visit www.greenwaysholidays.com,

email: tourism@planed.org.uk, or write to Greenways Holidays, The Old School, Station Road, Narberth, Pembrokeshire SA67 7DU.

Go Greenways

This year the Pembrokeshire Coast National Trail is fully accessible by public transport, thanks to the introduction of the Pembrokeshire Coastal Bus Services. Active locals and visitors can enjoy stress-free travel along the coastline and walkers can now walk the entire trail without having to use a car.

Pembrokeshire Coastal Buses are local bus services that enable you to travel along the Pembrokeshire coastline, 7 days a week, to access walks, beaches, boat trips, local villages and attractions.

Puffin Shuttle

St Davids - Milford Haven. The route passes through the beautiful sights of Newgale, Broad Haven, Little Haven, Marloes and Dale - so all you have to do is sit back and enjoy the ride!

Celtic Coaster

Around the St Davids Peninsula. The bus runs on Bio-diesel', an environmentally friendly fuel, and can also carry surfboards, 2 x bikes and 1 x wheelchair.

All aboard the Coastal Cruiser

The 14 seater minibus runs from St Davids to Port Clais, St Justinians and Whitesands, enabling you to walk the Peninsula, catch the boat trips to Ramsey Island or enjoy a day on the beach.

Strumble Shuttle

St Davids - Fishguard. The bus takes you to Aberiddi beach, Porthgain, Trefin, Mathry, Tregwynt Woollen Mill (for Porth Mawr beach), St Nicholas, Trefasser Cross (for Pwll Deri YHA) and as close to Strumble Head as we can get before taking you into Goodwick and Fishguard.

Poppit Rocket

Fishguard - Cardigan, calling at Pwllgwaelod, Newport, Moylegrove, Poppit Sands (for the start of the Coast Path) and St Dogmaels.

New Coastal Cruiser

This 'surf & bike' bus runs out of Pembroke to Angle, Bosherston, Stackpole and Freshwater East. The bus carries surfboards, 2 x bikes, 2 x wheelchairs and all your beach gear!

Look out for the buses that display the 'Puffin' logo and the eye-catching 'Puffin' bus stops - this means that they are part of the coastal bus services. Catching a bus in Pembrokeshire is easy. You don't even have to find the bus stop

because all coastal buses operate on a 'Hail & Ride' basis, so all you have to do is signal to the driver to stop. Passengers can be picked up or set down at any point along the bus route - providing it is safe to do so. Once on board your driver will have plenty of local knowledge to help you find your destination or recommend one!

The Coastal, Cruiser, Puffin Shuttle, Celtic Coaster, Poppit Rocket and Strumble Shuttle coastal bus services run 7 days a week during the holiday season, with a reduced service in the winter.

In the south of the county local bus services provide a year round service and between 19th July and 28th September a new 7 day bus service from Pembroke to Angle, Bosherston and Stackpole will be available.

NEW Preseli Hills walkers bus

If you are heading to the Preseli Hills this summer then look out for the new 'walkers' bus service, which starts running from Crymych on 30th April 2005.

The 'Preseli Green Dragon' bus is an important link for walkers on the Preseli Hills, providing transport to the start of the walk without having to use a car and enables you to enjoy walks, such as the 'Golden Road'

ridgeline, without re-tracing your steps - the perfect walking partner!

The bus route hugs the foothills from Crymych to Mynachlog-ddu, Maenclochog, Rosebush, Brynberian, Cilgwyn, Nevern and Newport. In addition to this the bus will also provide a service to Sychpant, in the Gwaun Valley.

This service will run two days a week on Tuesdays and Saturdays from Saturday 30th April to Saturday 1st October 2005.

Book your seat in advance. The bus will operate as a Dial–a–Ride service with passengers required to book a seat in advance. To book your seat please telephone 0800 783 1584 at least one hour before the bus is due to run. Details are also available from: www.prta.co.uk

Take the train for a walk!

This summer why not use the train to get yourself around Pembrokeshire. The Greenways 'Walk & Ride' leaflet details walks from Whitland, Narberth, Saundersfoot, Tenby, Manorbier, Lamphey, Haverfordwest and Milford Haven train stations. It also includes walks by bus in the Preseli Hills and St Dogmaels.

You can enjoy discounted travel with the 'Greenways Day Ranger' ticket, which enables you to have unlimited day travel along this stretch of line for just £3.50 (adults) or £1.75 (child), available from ticket conductors on Wales & West trains between Whitland and Pembroke Dock.

Pembrokeshire Greenways is a project that encourages people to access the countryside through walking, cycling, bus and train travel.

The Pembrokeshire Greenways Partnership is made up of all the organisations that deliver walking, cycling and public transport in Pembrokeshire and includes: Countryside Council for Wales, Environment Wales, National Trust, Pembrokeshire Access Group, Pembrokeshire Coast National Park Authority, Pembrokeshire County Council and PLANED.

If you want more information on where you can walk and cycle, or details of where you can get to by bus or train in Pembrokeshire then pick up a timetable or leaflet from any Tourist Information Centre or contact Kirsty Morris, Greenways Officer on 01437 776313 or visit the website at www.pembrokeshiregreenways.co.uk

The Coastal Cruiser

PEMBROKESHIRE'S ISLANDS & WILDLIFE

CARDIGAN ISLAND

A small island of less than 16 hectares, situated at the mouth of the River Teifi. The island is leased by The Wildlife Trust of South and West Wales, who annually census its small colonies of seabirds. The lesser black-backed gulls are the dominant species, with only a few hundred herring gulls and very small numbers of other seabirds. In 1934, when the motor vessel Herefordshire was wrecked on the northern rocks, brown rats came ashore and annihilated the island's population of puffins.

There have been various attempts to reinstate both puffins and Manx shearwaters; a few have bred but it is a long and slow process to establish healthy breeding colonies here again.

RAMSEY ISLAND

260 hectares of fascinating island, now accessible by a regular boat service from the lifeboat slip at St. Justinian's (about 3 miles west of St. Davids), across the infamous but spectacular Ramsey Sound, with its equally infamous and treacherous reef known as The Bitches.

Ramsey was farmed until very recently. To the east, steep sheltered spring-fed valleys and cliffs are covered in a wonderful tangle of rich vegetation, and to the north-east are sheep-grazed fields which support perhaps the largest population of breeding lapwings in Wales. Chough also find Ramsey extremely attractive, and both species breed and winter here in good numbers. The western coastline is rugged and spectacular, with two small mountains, (Carn Llundain and Carn Ysgubor) shelter-

Skomer in Spring

ing the island from the main blast of the prevailing westerly winds.

The Island is also home to several thousand seabirds in the season, including razorbills, kittiwakes, fulmars and guillemots.

On a clear day the mountain top views are superb. To the north and east are St. Davids and the Preseli Hills; to the west, the rocks and islets of the Bishops and Clerks, and the main South Bishop rock, where Manx shearwaters and storm petrels breed; and to the south, the small offshore islands of Ynys Cantwr and Ynys Beri, with Skomer and Midland Isle beyond them across St. Bride's Bay.

The caves and beaches around Ramsey are breeding grounds for the largest population of grey seals in south-western Britain; more than 300 seal pups are born here each season.

In 1992 the Royal Society for the Protection of Birds bought Ramsey. There is now a resident warden on the island, who meets every visitor, though there are necessary restrictions on the number of people allowed on the island each day. For those lucky enough to make it, there are refreshments and a shop. Unpaid assistant wardens can arrange to stay and help with work on the reserve.

GRASSHOLM

Currently the island of Grassholm is not open to the public, but a trip around the island remains a truly unforgettable experience.

Situated around eleven miles offshore, Grassholm is a reserve of the Royal Society for the Protection of Birds, and is the only Gannet colony in Wales. Viewed from afar the island appears to be snow

covered or having a white halo - this in fact is the Gannet colony. Approximately 30,000 pairs of Gannets crowd into the tiny, waterless island to lay their single egg.

The noise and sheer spectacle of vast numbers of these magnificent seabirds is something that once experienced will never be forgotten. Gannets are brilliant white in colour and dive for fish in the waters around Grassholm from heights up to 30 metres. When one realises that a full-grown Gannet is about the size of the average Christmas goose the spectacle becomes more amazing!

Writer Dr Brian John

Pembrokeshire's islands - a haven for a huge variety of wildlife

describes the scene thu "there can be few more beau tiful sights than Gannets div ing close inshore, wheelin and swooping on the brigh clean wind of Pembrokeshire summer day.

The second larges Gannet colony in Britain Grassholm is a major succes story. In 1924, there wer 1,000 pairs recorded on th island to an officially record ed 30,000 pairs in 1989.

Although Gannets domi nate the island to such degree that even from th mainland it has beer described as resembling ar iced bun, other breeding birds include small numbers

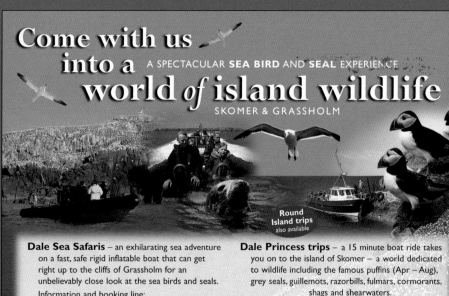

of Kittiwake, Razorbill, Shag together with Herring and Great Black-backed Gulls.

From the boats that take visitors around the island, there are often sightings of porpoise, basking shark and even the occasional sunfish; plus of course a variety of birds, such as Puffin or Shearwater, which may be resident on the other neighbouring islands.

SKOMER

This is the largest of Pembrokeshire's islands, a National Nature Reserve owned by the Countryside Council for Wales but run by The Wildlife Trust of South and West Wales, who employ a permanent warden and staff.

The island ferry runs from Martin's Haven, on the Marloes Peninsula, every day except Monday, though during bank holidays the island is open to visitors all the time. There is a charge for the boat trip and also for landing, but children under 16 are exempt from the latter.

There are guided tours around Skomer, usually operated by the National Park Authority, but in the main visitors are greeted and given a brief informative talk, which includes information on where to find all the island's interesting sights and wildlife. From then until the boats leave in the afternoon, you are free to explore via the well-defined footpaths.

Skomer has some very well preserved archaeological remains dating back to the early Iron Age, in the form of standing stones, hut circles, burial cairns, walls and numerous lynchets. The island was farmed until the mid-1950's, but is now grazed only by rabbits - albeit thousands of them! The flora is not rich but the carpets of spring and early summer flowering bluebells, red campion, white sea campion and thrift are some of the most colourful in the west.

The island's cliff scenery is spectacular, both scenically and for its many thousands of breeding guillemots, razorbills, kittiwakes and fulmars. More than 20,000 pairs of lesser black-backed gulls nest in the middle of the island - the largest colony of this species in Europe. Other gulls, such as greater black-backed and herring, are also well represented.

Skomer, in fact, boasts the largest colony of breeding seabirds in southern Britain. This is in spite of many years farming activity during which no species of ground predators - even rats or cats - ever managed to establish themselves. Hence ground and burrow nesting sites are numerous. There are over 6000 pairs of puffins and at least 165,000 pairs of Manx

Above: Caldey Island

Below: Pair of Guillemots, Skomer

shearwaters - the world's biggest colony. Of the ground-nesting birds, there are good numbers of short-eared owls, curlews and oystercatchers, to name but a few.

The Island is also home to a unique island race of bank voles, common shrews and wood mice, and on the beaches during the autumn over 150 grey seal pups are born, making this the second most important seal-breeding colony in south-western Britain. Another notable colony is that established by shags on Midland Island, a much smaller island south of Skomer.

Skomer, Grassholm and Skokholm are all included in a Special Protection Area designated by a European directive - a further indication of the value of Pembrokeshire's offshore islands to international wildlife.

SKOKHOLM

This small island has been owned by the Dale Castle Estates since the 1970's and is now leased by The Wildlife Trust of South and West Wales, who employ a cook and a warden. There is full-board accommodation for up to 16 people a week.

Skokholm has all the richness and profusion of wildlife and beauty of Skomer, but in a smaller, more gentle way. The only

seabird not common to bot is the kittiwake, and in th quarry on the westerly clifl below the lighthouse there i a colony of several thousanc storm petrels - the larges colony in the Irish Sea.

In 1936 the island was se up as Britain's first ever birc observatory by a group o people which includec Ronald (R.M.) Lockley. This of course, is Lockley's Drean Island, which was occupiec and farmed by him unti 1940.

ST. MARGARET'S ISLAND

St. Margaret's Island anc its much bigger neighbour Caldey, lay some way to the south of the county.

The island has the largest colony of cormorants in Wales, located on top of its steep limestone cliffs, while other seabirds include greater black-backed and herring gulls, guillemots, razorbills, kittiwakes and fulmars on the vertical cliffs. There are very few puffins, but burrow-nesting birds are restricted by the presence of rats.

The island and its wildlife, and the coastline of Caldey, are best seen from one of the pleasure boats, which run regularly from Tenby harbour between April and September, but no landings are allowed on St. Margaret's.

CALDEY

Caldey is owned and run by the small community of Cistercian monks, who farm the island with the help of a few people in the village.

A day out here is totally different from anything else you will experience in Pembrokeshire. Several boats a day take many curious visitors to this atmospheric and religious centre, and landings and access are simple compared to the other islands.

Leaving the boat you walk towards the village and monastery passing Priory Beach - a beautiful, gently curving stretch of sand backed by dunes, and the island,s only safe bathing beach. The easy stroll up through the trees has a distinctly Mediterranean feel to it, which is emphasised when you see the monastery.

The imposing but attractive monastic buildings are all whitewashed and have terra-cotta roofs. The village itself has everything to offer visitors including shops and a café with open-air seating under swaying, whispering trees.

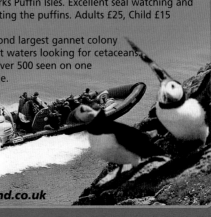

ISLAND BOAT TRIPS

Aquaphobia

The Ramsey Island Booking
Office in the grounds of the
Grove Hotel opposite the
Tourist Information Centre in
St. Davids
Tel: 01437 720471/721648

Caldey Island Boat Trips

Frequent boats from
Tenby Harbour.
Tel: 01834 844453/842296

Dale Sailing Company Ltd

Regular Island trips
Tel: 0800 0284090

Shearwater Safaris

Island trips
*Tel: 08081 445529/01437
781569*

Thousand Islands Expedition

Ramsey Island boat and fish
trips
Cross Square, St. Davids
Tel: 0800 163621

Voyages of Discovery

The Ramsey Island Boat
Booking Office opposite
Lloyds Bank in the centre
St. Davids
Tel: 0800 854367

*Above: Images Courtesy of
Janet Baxter*

THE GREAT SPORTING & ACTIVITY HOLIDAY

Health and fitness are increasingly important facets of modern lifestyles, and this is reflected in the growing number of visitors who come to Pembrokeshire in search of sporting and activity holidays.

Certainly, there is no better place to choose: with the only coastline in Britain designated a National Park, Pembrokeshire combines the best of the great outdoors with the very best in indoor leisure facilities.

The variety and quality of activities is second to none - whether visitors want to enjoy the sedate pleasure of bird watching or tackle the more taxing pursuits of surfing, canoeing, or climbing. Whatever you favour, it's all here in Pembrokeshire as the following guide illustrates.

EXPLORING PEMBROKESHIRE'S MAGICAL COASTLINE

A holiday in Pembrokeshire presents you with dozens of choices; too many sometimes. Trying to make decisions about where to go, what to do and keeping the whole family happy can interfere with actually getting on and doing! Some days you just need to get away, find somewhere new and leave the everyday world behind. If simply sitting on the beach is not an option, or the kids are demanding more things to keep them busy then TYF Coastal Explorer days fit the bill.

Rachel Allan, from Cardiff, came exploring with her family in the summer. "We have coasteered several times before and the Explorer days are a great extension to that – it is the perfect answer of packing the fun in whilst keeping holiday stress down"

Coastal Explorer days are just that, there is no fixed script to follow. The three elements to the day –kayaking, Coasteering® and snorkelling – all come with specialist equipment; you simply choose how wet to get and how far you want or need to go. Your TYF Adventure Guide will be with you showing, helping and teaching you about the most beautiful coastline in Britain; arguably in the world, as you paddle, dabble and scrabble your way along.

Sit-on-top kayaks are your chariot for the day and are a great way of covering the distance between launch and lunch. They are highly stable and run in a straight line so no need for exhaustive lessons or

Sit-on-top kayaks at TYF

frustrating circles. If you jump off for a swim you simply climb back on and get going again.

You will already have the kit with you for Coasteering® – TYF's premier adventure – so you can stretch your legs while playing in "Hogwart's" wave machine or running the gauntlet of "Judgement Day". Cliff jumping is close by too for those that want a quick adrenaline rush.

This coastal national park is as impressive under the water as it is up above. Wearing a diving mask and swimming or paddling around gives the feeling of flying across canyons and seaweed forests, with all sorts of weird and wonderful things normally unseen.

Lunch in a remote place is all a part of the deal and you'll certainly have raised an appetite by the time you pull your kayak from the water. The stories will start to flow, between mouthfuls of sandwich, everyone with a special moment.

For those that would "rather sit on the grass and watch", you may be tempted to wave goodbye to your adventurers at Twr y Felin hotel and then spoil yourself with a quick snack in the bar, before strolling down to the cliffs with your camera to capture the action. At the end of the day as the fisherman's stories get bigger you'll be sharing a glow and buzz coming from

spending a day out of door being active and sharing grea times. Finish with a celebra ory meal or just an ice-crea and then back to planning th rest of your week; no rest!

Details of the Coast Explorer and all TYF Adventu breaks are available at thei shops in St. Davids and Tenby, o the web - www.tyf.com - or k phoning 01437 721611.

ACTIVITY CENTRES

Activity Wales

Riverside Quay, Haverforc west. *Tel: 01437 766888* also a Gower House, Tudor Square Tenby, *Tel: 01834 844000*

One stop shops fo booking activities, accommo dation and travel.

Base Camp Outdoor Centre

Llawhaden, Narberth. Offers canoeing and kayaking climbing and abseiling, coast eering, biking, walking and hillwalking.

Tel: 01437 541318.

Celtic Diving

Main Street, Goodwick Offers diving, snorkeling courses, refresher dive, boa trips. *Tel: 01348 874752,*

Dive Pembrokeshire

The Dive Lodge, Old School House, Walton West Little Haven. RYA powerboa courses, diving, windsurfing

surfing and sailing.
Tel: 01437 781117.

Pembrokeshire Dive Charters

Brunel Quay, Neyland
Dive training centre aimed
at recreational divers.
Tel: 08081 445529

Pembrokeshire Water Sports

Cleddau River Centre,
Pembroke Dock. **Tel: 01646 622013** and The Parrog,
Fishguard. **Tel: 01348 874803**
The centre offers dinghy
sailing, windsurfing, power-
boating, canoeing, kayaking,
coasteering, and caters for
wheelchair students.

Preseli Venture

Mathry near St. Davids.
This centre offers adven-
ture weekends, sea kayaking,
coasteering, surfing, mountain
biking and walking.
Tel: 01348 837709.

The Prince's Trust

Dolphin Court, Brunel
Quay, Neyland. Here you can
enjoy canoeing and kayaking,
caving, climbing/abseiling,
coasteering, orienteering,
walking and hillwalking, and
caters for wheelchair users.
Tel: 01646 603130.

Sealyham Activity Centre

Wolfcastle, near Haver-
fordwest. Activities include
rock climbing and abseiling,
kayaking, surfing, coasteering,

mountain biking, archery,
dinghy sailing and assault
courses.
Tel: 01348 840763.

TYF No Limits Adventure

1, High Street, St. Davids.
Tel: 01437 721611 or St. Julians
Street, Tenby. **Tel: 01834 843488 or FREEPHONE 0800 132588:** adventure days, family
holidays, summer camps
combines kayaking, surfing,
climbing and abseiling, coasteering and working with the
environment.

West Wales Wind, Surf and Sailing

Dale
Canoeing, kayaking,
surfing, sailing, windsurfing
and power boats. Also caters
for wheelchair users.
Tel: 01646 636642.

BIRDWATCHING

Ardent twitchers or those
who just enjoy watching birds
can have the time of their lives
whatever the season. In winter,
the rivers Teifi, Cleddau and
Nevern are home to Little
Egrets, Slovonian Grebes and
Great Northern Divers
together with wildfowl waders.
Spring sees the arrival of
swallows, warblers and many
varieties of seabirds, while
inland Peregrine falcons,
Merlins, together with
Lapwings, Golden Plovers and
Buzzards take to the sky.

Windsurfing on the Cleddau estuary

The islands of Ramsey, Skomer and Grassholm offer the widest selection of birds including Fulmars, Kittiwakes, Guillemots, Razorbills and Puffins to name but a few. Skomer has the distinction of being home to the largest colony of Manx Shearwaters in the world, while Grassholm has the second largest colony of Gannets in the North Atlantic.

Elegug Stacks near Castlemartin also has large colonies of Guillemots, Razorbills and Kittiwakes, while the Welsh Wildlife Centre at Cilgerran near Cardigan is home to countless varieties of birds and wildfowl.

Both Skomer and Ramsey can be visited by boat. Skomer boats run daily (except Monday) from Martins Haven between April 1st or Easter (whichever is the sooner) until October 31st. Contact the Dale Sailing Company on *01646 603123.*

There are a number of boat operators who visit Ramsey - contact Aquaphobia on *01437 720471/721648,* Voyages of Discovery on *0800 854367* or Thousand Islands on *0800 163621,* or pick up leaflets locally.

A number of the boat operators also visit Grassholm, where you can't go ashore.

Vantage points for bird watching also include Amroth, Strumble Head near Fishguard, Nevern estuary, Cleddau Estuary, Carew Mill Pond, Fishguard Harbour, Westfield Pill at Neyland and Bosherston Pools near Pembroke.

CANOEING & KAYAKING

North Pembrokeshire's dramatic coastline offers just the sort of conditions ideal for canoeing and kayaking. For beginners there are quiet sheltered bays where even the complete novice soon feels at home, while the more expert can take up the challenge of tide races and overfalls. Beginners are often surprised to discover that even on their first trip, under the guidance of an experienced and qualified instructor, they begin to master the basic skills and are able to enjoy the thrills of exploring cliffs and sea caves and negotiating rocks and waves.

TYF No Limits Adventure

1, High Street, St. Davids. **Tel: 01437 721611** or St. Julians Street, Tenby. **Tel: 01834 843488 or FREEPHONE 0800 132588**

Pembrokeshire Watersports

The Cleddau River Centre, Pembroke Dock. **Tel: 01646 622013** and The Parrog, Fishguard. **Tel: 01348 874803**

CLIMBING

Pembrokeshire offers climbers of all abilities the opportunity to experience some of the finest sea-cliff climbing in the British Isles. The county's geographic location and mild winters mean all-year-round climbing on dry, warm rock - a treat rarely available in mountainous areas. So the area is very popular, especially during early bank holidays, and there may well be queues for some of the plum 3-star routes.

The sea cliffs are the home of many nesting birds, some of them rare and because of this very necessary restrictions have been imposed in certain areas from early February until mid-August. So climbers are advised to choose their routes carefully as it cannot be stressed too strongly that if climbers and wildlife are to co-exist successfully in this environmentally sensitive corner of Britain, the restrictions imposed must be adhered to. Further details of these restrictions are available from all National Park Information Centres in the county, and in the Climber's Guide to Pembrokeshire.

You should also remember that this hazardous coastline keeps the coastguard and rescue services fully occupied without any further help from stranded climbers, so at all times take every possible safety precaution, including the use of a helmet, because of the ever-present danger of loose rock.

The Pembrokeshire Coast was made for coasteering!

GIVING MO

With various activities, courses, clubs and classes at 11 leisure sites our qualified tea
ready to increase your fitness, health and well being in a fun, flexible and enjoyable

New site developments, extensive staff training and new management are just some
the changes which make Pembrokeshire Leisure key to giving us more in LIFE & LEIS

WHY EXERCISE?

Pembrokeshire Leisure is committed to providing high quality health and fitness related facilities, opportunities and specialist advice for its customers. We are concerned about the reported state of the Nations health and are committed to improve the health and fitness of the people of Pembrokeshire. The following information sets the scene for why we need to provide a first class service and what we can offer you to achieve your own personal goals.

The adoption of a more physical lifestyle can not only add years to your life but also improve the quality of your life, even if you have previously been inactive. There is increased evidence of the benefits of physical activity in relation to disease prevention, mobility, independence and quality of life. During the past decade Wales has seen some dramatic changes in the health of our nation. Obesity has increased and people are leading more inactive lifestyles.

Physical activity can play an important role in the management of our weight,

health, stress, blood pressure and fitness levels. This in turn can aid in the prevention life threatening illnesses such as heart disea diabetes and strokes.

Exercise is vitally important to keep our bodies in good working order. In today's modern world where we have machines to do everything, we do not always get the exercise we need to keep us healthy.

There are lots of benefits attached to regular exercise, including:

• improvements to our heart and lungs

• reduction in blood pressure

• maintaining and increasing bone density

• reducing cholesterol

• reducing the impact of ageing

• maintaining muscle strength and joint flexibility

RE TO
LIFE & LEISURE

Pembrokeshire Leisure
Hamden Sir Benfro

Pembrokeshire Leisure is committed to
GIVING MORE TO LIFE & LEISURE

ecial types of physical activity can:

significantly improve mobility and strength, which in turn helps to maintain independent living

• provide psychological benefits by improving moods and anxiety, leading to improved quality of life.

We are committed to providing resources to ncourage sport for all.

he aim of Pembrokeshire Leisure is to provide co-ordinated and consistent leisure service hat will increase levels of health and well-eing in Pembrokeshire through greater articipation and the delivery of enjoyable, ustomer-focused services.

The 'Pembrokeshire Leisure' network consists of 11 leisure facilities across Pembrokeshire, each one unique to the community it serves.

Joining one centre means you have access to each of the other centres throughout the County.

You may live in Tenby but work in Haverfordwest: 'Pembrokeshire Leisure' provides you with the freedom to use either centre at your convenience.

There are activities suitable for everyone, from young babies to the older members of the community.

Each centre offers a wide range of activities all aimed at promoting fitness, good health, general well being and ENJOYMENT!

Our aim is to make 'Pembrokeshire Leisure' as flexible as possible, to consistently meet the needs of our customers, and to give everybody the opportunity to lead a healthy life.

Call 01437 775461 for further Information

165

COASTEERING

Another growing sport is Coasteering, which is definitely an activity for the more daring. It involves a combination of climbing and scrambling along the rocky coastline, swimming and cliff jumping into the sea.

TYF No Limits Adventure

1, High Street, St. Davids. *Tel: 01437 721611* or St. Julians Street, Tenby. *Tel: 01834 843488 or FREEPHONE 0800 132588*

CYCLING & MOUNTAIN BIKING

There is no better way to enjoy the magnificence of the Pembrokeshire coastline and the beauty and tranquillity of the countryside than on a mountain bike - especially as the whole of the National Park is criss-crossed with a network of hidden tracks, bridle ways and sunken lanes. When cycling in Pembrokeshire it is very important to remember that the coast path is for walkers only - a law strictly enforced by the National Park Authority, who are responsible for maintaining this long distance footpath. Furthermore, off-road cyclists should at all times give way to walkers and horse riders, and be courteous and considerate to the farmers and landowners whose land they are crossing.

For cyclists who prefer to be on the road than off it Pembrokeshire has more quiet lanes than most people could cycle round in a lifetime. Touring in the county could hardly be easier, with bed and breakfast available round every corner and plenty of youth hostels within easy reach.

Mike's Bikes

17 Prendergast, Haverfordwest
Tel: 01437 760068

Preseli Venture

Mathry
Tel: 01348 837709
Tel: 01239 820905

DIVING

The natural beauty of Pembrokeshire with its picturesque countryside and dramatic scenery is mirrored in its underwater landscape. Diving is a very popular pastime with clubs from all over Britain visiting the clear water where hundreds of wrecks abound, and reefs offer a variety of fish life. Some of the dive sites are marine reserves so their inhabitants remain untouched. Seals often accompany divers as they explore the underwater world and if you're lucky enough, dolphins, porpoises and even sea horses have been

known to swim in certain areas, particularly around Cardigan Bay where a pod of dolphins are resident to the area. There are dive sites to suit all abilities - from novice to the more experienced diver.

Celtic Diving

Main Street, Goodwick
Tel: 01348 874752

Dive Pembrokeshire

The Dive Lodge, Little Haven, Haverfordwest.
Tel: 01437 781117

Pembrokeshire Dive Charters

Brunel Quay, Neyland
Tel: 08081 445529

West Wales Diving Centre

Hasguard Cross, Broadhaven
Tel: 01437 781457

West Wales Diving School

Sessions Hall, Mathry near Haverfordwest.
Tel/Fax 01348 831526

Celtic Diving

Sea Trust (a section of the Wildlife Trust, South and West Wales) has been up and running for just about a year now, with funding from Environment Wales, The Countryside Council for Wales (CCW) and, more recently, Stena Line. We can now begin to appraise our performance against the goals we set out to achieve.

Sea trust began primarily as a group of people united in their concern for their local marine environment. We felt that our local knowledge, observations and records gained over the years, could and should be shared with decision makers to help preserve and conserve our marine environment.

Therefore the aims of Sea Trust are to promote awareness of the marine environment and its biodiversity amongst the community.

Photos: Mark Deane
www.celticdiving.co.uk

Our porpoise surveys at Strumble head have evolved from relatively naive casual records to really quite sophisticated recording methodology. Using a dedicated colour coded form, porpoise presence and activity is recorded in 15 minute periods over an hour. These forms can be added together to record consecutive hours.

Data recorded includes climatic and tidal conditions, presence of porpoises (and other animals), estimates of numbers present, also seabird and boat activity. Position of animals and activity is also plotted on the accompanying chart, as is the prevailing tiderace. Mothers and calves are noted and also activity such as breaching etc.

These records have established that porpoises are present year round at Strumble and also breed in the vicinity. Bottlenose dolphins are frequently seen in Fishguard and Newport Bays during the summer but are hardly ever recorded at Strumble (only a couple of miles away).

Other species of dolphin such as common and Risso's, though by no means common turn up annually. In the case of common dolphins, sightings have only occurred in the past decade from Strumble and have increased. This may have something to do with observer time expanding but we think not entirely. A single striped dolphin was recorded with commons but is the only record I am aware of.

Risso's have been recorded from June through to January with a handful of sightings most years. Occasionally we have had the mind-blowing experience of watching mothers with very young calves pass close by, a really exquisite experience.

Orcas, Minke's and larger Rorquals have also been recorded but only a handful.

More information on the local conservation group 'Sea Trust' can be obtained from; www.seatrust.org.uk

Editorial Text: Cliff Benson www.seatrust.org.uk

For more information and news on our activities and courses please visit our homepage; www.celticdiving.co.uk

FISHING

Whether you are looking for an out-and-out fishing holiday or you simply want to enjoy a bit of fishing while you're here, Pembrokeshire and West Wales provide wonderful opportunities for sea, game and coarse fishing.

The coastlines of Pembrokeshire, Cardigan Bay and Carmarthen Bay are excellent venues for summer sea angling, either from beaches or from established rock marks. Bass, pollack, garfish, mackerel, conger eel and even tope are all here for

he taking, while if you want to fish offshore, there is no shortage of charter boats offering fishing trips from local harbours.

West Wales has long been renowned for the quality of its game fishing, with most of the area's rivers and their tributaries experiencing good runs of salmon and sea trout during the summer months. Indeed, the region boasts three of Britain's premier salmon rivers - the Towy, Teifi and Taf - and many others provide terrific sport when conditions are favourable. These include the Nevern, Aeron, Eastern Cleddau, Western Cleddau, Rheidol and Ystwyth.

Wales also has an abundance of lakes and reservoirs that are well stocked with brown and rainbow trout. Venues popular with visitors are the reservoirs at Llys-y-fran Country Park and Rosebush (both close to the B4329, about 6 miles northeast of Haverfordwest), White House Mill and Latch y Goroff (near Whitland), and the trout fisheries of Llwyndrissi, Llanllawddog and Garnffrwd (near Carmarthen).

For coarse anglers, there are exciting prospects at a variety of locations. Bosherston lakes offer excellent pike fishing, and Llyn Carfan Lake at Tavernspite, between Red Roses and Whitland, boasts top-class carp fishing and a good head of tench and roach. Glas Llyn fishery near Blaenwaen is also stocked with carp and tench.

But remember, anybody aged 12 or over who fishes for salmon, trout, freshwater fish or eels in England and Wales must have an Environment Agency rod fishing licence, available from the Post Office or Environment Agency offices. In addition, you must have permission of the fishery owner before you may fish on waters under his or her control, and remember to take your litter home, as discarded tackle can injure wildlife.

Penrallt Nursery Moylegrove

Small lake well stocked with Rainbow Trout and situated in a pretty, peaceful setting with spectacular views of the coastline and hills. There is also a picnic area, children's play area and plant nursery and garden centre. Dogs welcome.

For further information, ring 01239 881295

Llys-y-Fran Reservoir and Country Park

Near Rosebush.
Tel: 01437 532273 or 532694

PEMBROKESHIRE COAST NATIONAL PARK

Over 50 years ago Pembrokeshire's outstanding coastline became a National Park - the highest designation a landscape can enjoy.

It is Britain's only predominantly coastal National Park and has one of the largest densities of protected environmental sites in Europe.

Rugged cliffs and islands, tree-lined estuaries around the Haven Waterway and Daugleddau and Preseli moorland are all features of the Park area. Wild flowers - spectacular on the coast in spring time - flourish in the mild climate and the seabird and seal colonies are world famous.

Man's hand upon this special landscape is there for all to see - from Iron Age hill forts and Neolithic burial chambers to imposing Norman castles and Victorian-era fortifications.

A splendid way to enjoy the Pembrokeshire Coast is to walk the Coast Path - one of Britain's cherished National Trails - stretching for an unbroken 186 miles from St Dogmaels in the north-east to Amroth in the south.

The Coast Path is just part of the access opportunities offered by the Park Authority which also maintains nearly 500 miles of inland paths.

The Pembrokeshire Coast is a walker's paradise - check out the Park's website: www.pembrokeshirecoast.org.uk for further information on walks or telephone 0845 345 7275.

FLYING

If taking to the skies is more your fancy then Haverfordwest Airport is the place to head for. There they have a Flying School for both aeroplanes and helicopters together with a Microlight Centre.

For further information, ring 01437 760822

GOLF

Tenby Golf Club

Tenby hosts the oldest golf club in Wales where The Burrows offers a superb 18-hole links course that regularly hosts events such as the Welsh National Championships. Overlooking Caldey Island, the clubhouse has a cordon bleu restaurant together with bar, lounge and snooker room.

Tel: 01834 842978

Trefloyne Golf Course

Trefloyne is a family owned golf course, located in the small village of Penally just outside Tenby. Trefloyne offers guests an 18 hole challenging parkland course set in mixed woodlands, with breath taking views over Carmarthen Bay and Caldey Island.

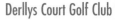

The focus of Trefloyne is pure and simple, a relaxed atmosphere with a warm friendly welcome. You don't have to be a golfer to enjoy the bar and restaurant.

Whether you have been out for the full 18, enjoyed a long walk through the woods or just wanted a lazy lunch with friends, Trefloyne really can cater for everyone.

See our website for further details www.trefloyne.com

Derllys Court Golf Club

A delightful 9 hole tree lined course of parkland nature, set in beautiful Carmarthenshire countryside with easy access off the bypass between Carmarthen and St Clears. The two lakes on the course afford a natural haven for an abundance of wildlife. The par 35 is of average length and the subtle nature of the course demands a great deal of driving accuracy. The clubhouse provides changing and shower facilities and easy access for the handicapped. Along with a licensed bar, snacks and meals are available during opening hours.

2004 saw the opening of a new 9 holes.

For more information ring 01267 211575

St. Davids City Golf Club

Established in 1902, this is one of the oldest golf clubs in Wales, and certainly the most westerly. The all weather links course is playable all year round and with the added attraction of stunning views over the bay and St. Davids Head, it is not surprising that this 6000-yard par 70 course is so popular with visitors.

For more information ring the clubhouse on 01437 721751 or ring the secretary on 01437 720058

On the other side of the waterway are two first-class 18-

hole courses at Haverfordwest and Milford Haven.

South Pembrokeshire Golf Club

This 18 hole hillside course is located at Pembroke Dock, on an elevated site overlooking the River Cleddau and the beautiful Haven Waterway.

There is always a warm welcome in the clubhouse, with an excellent restaurant and bar, which also have panoramic views of the Haven.

The club is only five minutes drive from the Irish Ferries Terminal at Pembroke Dock.

For more information ring Jeremy Tilson, Professional, on 01646 682442 or e-mail: spgc@supanet.com

Haverfordwest Golf Club

Haverfordwest Golf Club, formed in 1904, is situated on the outskirts of the town. The 18 hole course is a challenging one offering fabulous views of the Preseli Hills.

Tel: 01437 764523

Milford Haven Golf Club

A superb 18 hole par 71 meadowland course, with panoramic views of the Haven Waterway.

Tel: 01646 697762

Priskilly Forest Golf Club

Priskilly Forest near Letterston is a nine hole course set in mature parkland

Derllys Court Golf Club

SOUTH PEMBROKESHIRE GOLF CLUB

This 18 hole hillside course is located at Pembroke Dock, on an elevated site overlooking the River Cleddau and the beautiful Haven Waterway. The Clubhouse, Restaurant and Bar also have panoramic views. Meals are available at the clubhouse most days from early breakfast to evening meals. Individual, corporate memberships and daily visitors green fees all available at attractive rates. Booking is advisable to avoid disappointment. Ring 01646 682442. The club is only five minutes drive from the Irish Ferries Terminal at Pembroke Dock.

Military Road, West Pennar, Pembroke Dock SA72 6SE Tel: 01646 621453 (Secretary)

and only a ten minute drive from the Stena ferry terminal at Fishguard.

Tel: 01348 840276

Freystrop Golf Course

Freystrop in Haverford-west is a nine hole pay and play course in a lovely woodland setting, an added attraction of which is an all weather driving range. Restaurant facilities available.

Tel: 01437 764300

Rosemarket Golf Course

Rosemarket offers a challenging and very long nine hole parkland course cursed with numerous sand and water hazards to test players. An added unusual feature is a bookable grass landing strip offering a fly-drive with a difference!

Heatherton & Heron's Brook Golf Courses

Other golf courses include the one at St. Florence, an 18 hole pitch and putt course situated at the Heatherton Sports Park *Tel: 01646 651025*, and the 18 and nine hole courses at the Heron's Brook Leisure Park, Narberth.

Tel: 01834 860723 or 860023

Newport Golf Club

Newport Golf Club & Dormy House Holiday Flats: here you have a golf course which overlooks the magnifi-cent coastline of Newport Bay and superbly appointed holiday flats which overlook both! The interesting 9-hole par 35 links course is a challenge to players of all standards. The clubhouse offers full catering facilities and the self-catering flats adjoin the clubhouse and sleep up to 4 people.

Tel: 01239 820244

HORSE RIDING

With its lush countryside, quiet lanes, bridle paths and spectacular beaches, Pembrokeshire has the ideal environment for riding, which has long been a very popular leisure pursuit all over the county. There are a number of riding stables catering for visitors, and you can even book a riding or pony trekking holiday. But if you prefer being a spectator to being in the saddle, there are many events and shows to see, including gymkhanas, show jumping and point-to-point.

Bowlings Riding School

Meadow Farm, Rudbaxton, Haverfordwest.
Tel: 01437 741599

Crosswell Horse Agency

Velindre, Crymych.
Tel: 01239 891262

The Dunes Riding Centre
Martletwy, Narberth

A visit to Pembrokeshire wouldn't be complete without sampling the horse riding at the Dunes Riding Centre, near Oakwood. A friendly, family run stables offering riding for all abilities from complete beginners to those wanting a more adventurous ride.

Their fit, forward going horses and ponies will take you through woodland and forestry at a pace to suit your ability, ranging from an hour for the inexperienced, to a half day for the competent rider who can walk, trot and canter. Nervous riders and children can be led on the 1 hour ride which is suitable for novices from 5 to 75!

All prices include the use of approved riding hats and jodphur boots, and it is essential to book in advance. All rides are accompanied by cheerful competent escorts who will make this an experience to remember and cherish.

Phone them on 01834 891398 to sample the pleasure of horse riding with the experts!

East Nolton Riding Stables
Nolton, Haverfordwest.
Tel: 01437 710360

East Tarr Riding Stables
St. Florence, Tenby
Tel: 01834 871274

Heatherton Country Sports Park
St. Florence, Tenby.
Tel: 01646 651025

Llanwnda Stables
Penrhiw Fach, Llanwnda, Goodwick. *Tel: 01348 873595*

Maesgwynne Riding Stables
Fishguard
Tel: 01348 872659

Pembrokeshire Riding Centre
Pennybridge Farm, Hundleton, Pembroke.
Tel: 01646 682513

Horse riding along Pembrokeshire's country roads

THE GREAT SPORTING AND ACTIVITY HOLIDAY

Sycamores Ranch Western Riding Centre, near Llawhaden, Narberth

Have you ever dreamed of riding a western horse out on the American plains but thought it was either too expensive or too far to travel? Well Sycamores Ranch in Llawhaden near Narberth can offer you this experience here in beautiful Wales. The conformable saddles, well behaved horses, idyllic scenery all add up to an opportunity not to be missed.

The Ranch caters for people from the average to the more experienced rider and offer from 1 hour to whole day trails with barbecue. The trails include riding along quiet off-road bridle paths to crossing rivers, streams and fords. Passing through the delightful Pembrokeshire countryside you will also come across many historic monuments, ranging from ancient castles to traditional Welsh farmhouses and picturesque churches.

We also arrange night rides in the summer months. These consist of leaving the Ranch early evening and riding out to a stop off point where a meal is provided and then riding back to the Ranch in time to put the horses to bed!

As well as the trail side we also teach people Western riding for those who want to take it a bit more seriously and we also take in horses for backing and schooling in western.

The Ranch also has it's beautiful American Quarter Horse stallion standing at stud and a Western Tack Shop which has possibly the largest selection of Western Tack from saddles to Stetsons, in Wales.

So come and give it a try!

For further information, contact Nick Evans on 0707 930 8941 or by emailing him at info@sycamoresranch.com or you can visit their website at www.sycamoresranch.com

Riding at Sycamores Ranch

KARTING

BP Karting
County Showground, Withybush, Haverfordwest. **Tel: 01437 769555**

Carew Karting
Carew Airfield, Sageston, Nr. Tenby **Tel: 01559 384078 or 07974 540689**

Kartrax
St. Davids Road, Letterston **Tel: 01348 840447**

QUAD BIKING

Ritec Valley Buggies
All-Terrain Vehicles, Ritec Valley Buggies, Penally near Tenby. **Tel: 01834 843390 See our advert on page 30.**

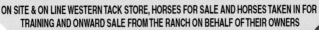

SAILING

Traditionally, dinghy sailing is very popular all over Pembrokeshire and southwest Wales. Yacht clubs such as Newport, Fishguard and Solva in the north of the county, and Tenby and Saundersfoot in the south, offer a friendly club atmosphere and a variety of facilities and racing programmes. Along the Milford Haven waterway - perhaps the most popular sailing location because it is sheltered from the open sea - you will find some of the larger and more active clubs, such as Neyland, Pembroke Haven, Pembrokeshire (Gelliswick, Milford Haven), and Dale.

For yachtsmen, the Haven has 22 miles of navigable inland waterway, with the additional challenge of exciting offshore sailing to the nearby islands of Skomer, Skokholm and Grassholm.

There are marinas at Milford Haven and Neyland, pontoons at Dale, Angle, Burton and Neyland, and various mooring sites all along the waterway.

Dale Yacht Club
Tel: 01646 636362

Milford Marina
Tel: 01646 692272

Neyland Marina
Tel: 01646 601601

Pembrokeshire Yacht Club
Gelliswick, Milford Haven.
Tel: 01646 692799

Pembrokeshire Cruising
Neyland Marina,
Brunel Quay, Neyland.
Tel: 01646 602500

Pembrokeshire Watersports
The Cleddau River Centre,
Pembroke Dock.
Tel: 01646 622013 and
The Parrog, Fishguard.
Tel: 01348 874803

Solva Sailboats
Trinity Quay, Solva.
Tel: 01437 720972

West Wales Wind, Surf & Sailing
Dale, Nr. Haverfordwest
Tel: 01646 636642

SURFING & WINDSURFING

Big waves, clear blue unpolluted waters, no crowds, and relatively mild air and water temperatures - the tempting combination which Pembrokeshire offers to surfers who are willing to travel that little bit further in order to stand out from the rest. Late summer and early autumn are particularly good times to take advantage of the county's superb beaches and surfing conditions.

Freshwater West, in South

Pembrokeshire, boasts the biggest and most consistent waves in the whole of Wales, with a variety of breaks to choose from. However, there are strong currents and no lifeguards, so beginners should not surf here. Other beaches worth checking out nearby include Broad Haven (south), Freshwater East and Manorbier. In North Pembrokeshire, good surfing can be enjoyed at Whitesands Bay, Newgale, Broad Haven and West Dale.

Age is no barrier to windsurfing, which attracts enthusiasts from 8 to 80. Some enjoy setting sail in light winds for a tranquil afternoon's cruise; others like to display their competitive streak by racing; and the most adventurous long for the exhilaration of strong winds and wave jumping in breaking surf.

Another big attraction of windsurfing is that it is easy to learn - provided you have the right equipment and tuition. One of Britain's top windsurfing and sailing venues is Dale. Its mile-wide bay promises superb sea sailing on flat water, with no strong tidal currents, and is ideal for beginners and experts alike. West Wales Windsurfing, Sailing and Canoeing, as

described in the section on sailing, is based on Dale waterfront and is a specialist watersports centre approved by the Royal Yachting Association. The expert tuition available here caters for everyone, from absolute beginner to advanced windsurfer. All equipment is provided, including wetsuits and buoyancy aids, and every instructor holds a nationally recognised qualification.

As for recommending the best beaches, Broad Haven (St. Bride's Bay) and Newgale are ideal for more experienced windsurfers (except in particularly calm conditions), whereas beginners and intermediates will breeze along more easily at Tenby, Saundersfoot, Newport and Fishguard.

SURF SHOPS & HIRE:

Haven Sports
Broadhaven *Tel: 01437 781354*

Ma Sime's Surf Hut
St. Davids. *Tel: 01437 720433*

Newsurf
Newgale Filling Station, Newgale. *Tel: 01437 721398*

Seaweed Surf Shop
Quay Street, Haverfordwest. *Tel: 01437 760774*

TYF No Limits Adventure
1, High Street, St. Davids. *Tel: 01437 721611* or St. Julians Street, Tenby. *Tel: 01834 843488 or FREEPHONE 0800 132588*

Underground Surf & Skate
4, Church Street, Tenby. *Tel: 01834 844234*

Waves 'n' Wheels
Commons Road, Pembroke. *Tel: 01646 622066*

The Windsurf Shop
Dale *Tel: 01646 636903*

PEMBROKESHIRE
LEISURE

Pembrokeshire Leisure
Hamden Sir Benfro

Facilities
- Swimming pools
- Teaching pools
- Swimming pool viewing areas
- Sports halls which facilitates badminton, football, volleyball, hockey and various other sports
- Health suites - spa bath, steam room and sauna
- Fitness suites
- Dance studios

- Coffee bars
- Disabled access & facilities
- Outdoor tennis courts
- Squash courts
- Bowls halls
- Sauna and steamrooms
- Recreation rooms
- Creches
- Full size all weather pitch
- All weather athletic track
- Seated vending areas

FREE SWIMMING
Over 60's are entitled to **FREE** entry into all public swimming sessions

ACTIVITY FOR LIFE
FOR LEISURE, HEALTH, FITNESS & WELL BEING

Call 01437 775461 for further Information

PEMBROKESHIRE LEISURE

Pembrokeshire Leisure Centre
Bush, Pembroke
Pembrokeshire SA71 4RJ
Tel: 01646 684434   Fax: 01646 621633

Haverfordwest Sports Centre
Sir Thomas Picton School Site, Queensway,
Haverfordwest, Pembrokeshire SA61 2NX
Tel: 01437 765901   Fax: 01437 768986

Pembrokeshire Water Sports & Conference Facility
Cleddau Reach, Pembroke Dock
Pembrokeshire SA72 6UJ
Tel: 01646 622013   Fax: 01646 681445

Haverfordwest Tennis and Cricket Centre
Tasker Milward School, Scarrowscant Lane
Haverfordwest SA611EP
Tel: 01437 765901   Fax: 01437 768986

St. Davids Swimming Pool
Ysgol Dewi Sant, St Davids
Pembrokeshire SA62 6QH
Tel: 01437 721898   Fax: 01437 721898

Fishguard Leisure Centre
Heol Dyfed, Fishguard
Pembrokeshire SA65 9DT
Tel: 01348 874514   Fax: 01348 874514

Narberth Swimming Pool
The Old School Grounds, Station Road, Narberth,
Pembrokeshire SA67 7DU
Tel: 01834 860940   Fax: 01834 869146

Crymych Leisure Centre
Crymych
Pembrokeshire SA41 3QH
Tel: 01239 831820   Fax: 01239 831964

Milford Leisure Centre
Priory Road, Milford Haven
Pembrokeshire SA73 2EE
Tel: 01646 694011   Fax: 01646 694453

Tenby Leisure Centre
Marsh Road, Tenby
Pembrokeshire SA70 8EJ
Tel: 01834 843575   Fax: 01834 845910

Thornton Sports Centre
Milford Haven
SA73 1AE
Tel: 01646 694011   Fax: 01646 694453

Call 01437 775461 for further Information

Creative Café,
Narberth

PEMBROKESHIRE'S ARTS & CRAFTS

Pembrokeshire is well known for its wealth of creative talent with an array of arts and crafts as diverse as the landscape. So whether it's candle making, wood turning, paintings or pottery you're after, you will find it all here in fabulous Pembrokeshire. The following is a brief guide to just some of the many attractions to be found across the county.

TENBY & THE SOUTH COAST

Art Matters
South Parade, Tenby
Tel: 01834 843375
A wide variety of quality original art in West Wales promoting the work of new and established artists.

Augustus Galleries
St. Georges Street, Tenby
Tel: 01834 845164/842204
A collection which includes some 250 paintings, drawings and prints by distinguished 19th/20th century artists.

Equinox
St Julian's Street, Tenby
Tel: 01834 843873
A fascinating collection of gifts and crafts.

Gift of Glass
Corner Trafalgar & Upper Park Road, Tenby
Tel: 01834 845886
Hand crafted glassware and gifts. Free glassblowing demonstrations.

Harbour View Ceramic Café
3 Crackwell Street, Tenby
Tel: 01834 845968 or
36 Blue Street, Carmarthen
Tel: 01267 229103
Paint your own pottery - explore your creative talent in a relaxed, fun atmosphere

Henry's Gift & Coffee Shop
5 Main Street, Pembroke
Tel: 01646 622293
An Aladdin's cave for those seeking quality gifts and local memorabilia.
See advert on page 46

Tenby Museum & Art Gallery
Castle Hill, Tenby
Tel: 01834 842809
Established in 1878, this national award-winning museum situated on a spectacular site overlooking Carmarthen Bay has two art galleries with regular changing exhbitions including a pemanent collection of work by local artists such as Gwen John, Augustus John, David Jones and John Piper.
Open throughout the year; daily during the summer season, and on week days,

from January to Easter. Full
access for disabled visitors.
Admission charges and concessions apply.

HAVERFORDWEST & THE WEST COAST

Andrew G. Bailey

23 Riverside Quay,
Haverfordwest
Tel: 01437 766889
Original watercolours, prints
and cards by the artist
together with a variety of
Pembrokeshire made crafts.

Celtic Images Gallery

Hilton Court Gardens, Roch,
Haverfordwest
Tel: 01348 837116
A showcase for
Pembrokeshire's top photo-
graphic and artistic talent.

The Old Smithy

Simpson Cross,
Haverfordwest
Tel: 01437 710628
Welsh crafts, gifts and new
purpose-built gallery showing
local artists.
See advert on page 80

Oriel Wilsons Gallery

7-11 Riverside Arcade,
Haverfordwest
Tel: 01437 760318
Original work by
Pembrokeshire artists.
See advert on page 77

The Sheep Shop

32 Bridge Street,
Haverfordwest
Tel: 01437 766844
Great range of gifts including
crafts, lovespoons, prints, etc.
See advert on page 77

ST. DAVIDS & THE NORTH COAST

Carningli Centre

East Street, Newport
Tel: 01239 820724
Art gallery, antiques show-
room, interesting collectables.

Harbour Lights Gallery

Porthgain, Nr St. Davids
Tel: 01348 831549
The best of Pembrokeshire
art is featured in this
harbourside gallery.

Jim Harries Woodturner

Mathry
Tel: 01348 831379
See the woodturner at work.
Interesting gifts and furniture.

Oriel-y-Felin Gallery & Tearoom

Trefin, nr St. Davids
Tel: 01348 837500
A constantly changing
selection of paintings,
ceramics, cards and prints.
See advert on page 107

*Original artwork by
Pauline Beynon at
Oriel-Y-Felin Gallery*

*Top:
"Autumn Moorland"*

*Above:
"Birds above the bay"*

185

PEMBROKESHIRE'S ARTS & CRAFTS

Laugharne Glass

FOLK ART IN THE TŶ BACH

Time plays tricks. Something that might seem ordinary in its own time can become valued, even unique by virtue of age and a change of ways. A recent discovery at Oriel-y-Felin is such an example. At the bottom of the garden is an old earth closet, a tŷ bach - in Welsh, literally, a "small house" - and its walls are covered with drawings of late 19th Century and early 20th Century sailing vessels. It's an incredible record of the ships sailed by a past owner of the house, Captain John George and his son Gwylim. Conservationists from the National Museum of Welsh Life are helping to preserve the drawings and visitors to the gallery can see them by request. Perhaps time moved more slowly back then - and more of it could be spent in the small house!

Pembrokeshire Candle Centre

Cilgwyn, Newport
Tel: 01239 820470
An Aladdin's cave of candles, candlesticks and candle - related items.

Solva Woollen Mill

Middle Mill, Solva
Tel: 01437 721112
A working mill weaving carpets and floor rugs.

INLAND PEMBROKESHIRE

Creative Café

Spring Gardens, Narberth
Tel: 01834 861651
Paint your own pottery. Choose from over 200 items, plenty of help and ideas provided - no artistic skill necessary!
See advert on page 134

Fabric House

6 High Street, Narberth
Tel: 01834 861063
Interiors and gifts for home and friends.
See advert on page 131

Furious Fish

14 Market Square, Narberth
Tel: 01834 861722
Contemporary jewellery combining precious and semi-precious metals and stones.
See advert on page 133

The Golden Sheaf Gallery

25 High Street, Narberth
Tel: 01834 860407
An innovative selection of art, crafts and gifts.
See advert on page 132

Haulfryn

13 High Street, Narberth
Tel: 01834 861902
Unusual, hand-made jewellery, antique silver, jewellery repairs.
See advert on page 131

Queens Hall Gallery

High Street, Narberth

Tel: 01834 861212
Exhibitions by local and other artists, situated in one of Pembrokeshire's top arts and entertainment venues.

The Slate Workshop
Pont Hywel Mill, Llangolman, Clunderwen
Tel: 01994 419543
By the side of the Eastern Cleddau River, at Llangolman, near Clunderwen.

Inspired by the lovely surroundings and by Celtic themes, Richard and Fran Boultbee produce fine lettering and designs in Welsh slate for house nameplates, plaques, memorials, sundials and clocks.

Richard sculpts the slate into wonderful tactile pieces and in the showroom their meticulously - finished craft items such as vases, bookends, cheeseboards and tealight holders are on sale.

CEREDIGION
Middle Earth
Priory Street, Cardigan
Tel: 01239 614080
Colourful, bohemian gifts and crafts from around the world.
See advert on page 210

Tŷ Custom House
44 St. Mary Street, Cardigan
Tel: 01239 615541
Shop and Gallery - Art, contemporary design, exclusive home accessories.

CARMARTHENSHIRE
Glyn Coch Studios
Pwll Trap, St. Clears
Tel: 01994 231867
Everything from art to wool, including clothes, jewellery, wood, iron and more, all made in Wales. See pottery being made - or make and decorate it yourself.
See advert on page 221

Laugharne Glass Studio
Market Square, Laugharne
Tel: 01994 427476
Originators of silver ornamented glass and glass blowing demonstrations.

Oriel Myrddin Gallery
Church Lane, Carmarthen
Tel: 01267 222775
See advert on page 215

World of Wales
3 Market Street, Laugharne
Tel: 01994 427632
An authentic range of Welsh crafts and gifts set in a relaxed old world atmosphere

Pembroke Glassblowing
The Commons, Pembroke
Tel: 01646 682482
Watch the hot glass worked into a wide range of imaginative gift ideas.
A fascinating craft
Viewing is free
See advert on page 42

The Slate Workshop

Manorbier Castle

PEMBROKESHIRE'S CASTLES & MUSEUMS

Pembrokeshire is not only rich in beautiful scenery; it also has more than its fair share of historic castles and ancient sites together with museums to suit visitors of all ages.

CAREW CASTLE

Carew is one of Pembrokeshire's finest castles with a wealth of detail and atmosphere. Owned and administered by the Pembrokeshire National Park Authority, to get there take the A477 from Pembroke Dock; or the Haverfordwest to St. Clears Road, then turn off the A4075.
Tel: 01646 651782

Carew Castle

CILGERRAN CASTLE

Cilgerran Castle is the most northerly castle in Pembrokeshire. Built with its ramparts overlooking cliffs on two sides, it was the favourite subject for the artist Turner. Owned by the National Trust and administered by CADW (Welsh Historical Monuments), it can be reached either along the A478 from Narberth or the A484 from Newcastle Emlyn then, follow the CADW signs.
Tel: 01239 615007

HAVERFORDWEST CASTLE

Haverfordwest Castle which overlooks the town, was once used as a prison, and more recently as a police station. Owned and administered by Pembrokeshire County Council, it now houses a small museum and the County Records Office.
Tel: 01437 763087

LLAWHADEN CASTLE

Llawhaden is one of the Landsker castles along the Landsker line, which is claimed to have divided North and South Pembrokeshire. It fell into disrepair in the mid 16th Century after being used as a bishop's residence. Owned and administered by CADW, it can be reached via the A40 from Haverfordwest or St. Clears, then the B4313.
Tel: 02920 500200

MANORBIER CASTLE

Manorbier Castle is where the BBC filmed part of the children's series "The Lion, the Witch and the Wardrobe". Set in a stunning area, it can be reached off the A4139 five miles from Tenby.
Tel: 01834 871394

189

NARBERTH CASTLE

Narberth Castle was built in the 13th Century, its most notable Castellan being Sir Rhys ap Thomas who was given the castle by Henry Vlll but by the 17th Century it had fallen into ruins, the remnants of which can be seen today.

NEVERN CASTLE

Very little remains of the castle but it provides an interesting view of the siting and layout of early medieval fortifications. To get there follow the Cardigan Road out of Fishguard. Once past Newport follow the signs to Nevern.

Picton Castle

NEWPORT CASTLE

Newport Castle is another that is in private ownership and not open to the public.

Pembroke Castle

PEMBROKE CASTLE

Pembroke Castle is one of the best-preserved medieval castles in Wales. Open to visitors all year round it is an intriguing place to explore. The wide walls are honeycombed with a seemingly endless system of rooms, passageways and spiralling flights of narrow stone steps; interpretative displays and information panels give a fascinating insight into the castle's origins and long

history. One of the mo impressive features is th distinctive round keep, whic was built soon after 1200. It 75 feet high and the viev from the top in all directior are nothing less tha magnificent.

Tel: 01646 681510 or 684585

PICTON CASTLE

Picton Castle is privatel owned and open to the publi six days a week. The beautifull laid out 40 acres of woodlan gardens are well worth a visi The castle lies three miles eas of Haverfordwest.

Tel: 01437 751326.
See advert on page 78

ROCH CASTLE

Roch Castle is also a pri vate residence. It is situated or the A487 from Haverfordwes to St. Davids.

WISTON CASTLE

Although very little remains, the castle is worth a visit if only to see the remains of the shell keep built to help protect the motte and bailey castle. Owned by CADW, it can be reached from Haverford-west, by taking the A40 towards Carmarthen and turning off at Wiston.

Tel: 02920 500200

Picton Castle

Pembroke Castle

CARREG SAMSON

Situated in the coastal village of Abercastle, Carreg Samson is a Neolithic Cromlech overlooking the picturesque fishing village. To get there follow the A487 St. Davids Road from Fishguard and then the signs to Abercastle.

CASTELL HENLLYS

Castell Henllys is the site of an Iron Age Fort, which has been recreated using authentic materials and techniques. To get there take the A487 from Fishguard to Cardigan, and look for the signs.

HAVERFORDWEST TOWN MUSEUM

Haverfordwest Town Museum is situated in the castle overlooking the town, and has been created to illustrate the history of the area. It houses exhibits explaining the castle and prison, which were once housed there, and the transport and industry into the town together with the institutions and personalities that make up Haverfordwest.

Tel: 01437 763087

LAMPHEY BISHOP'S PALACE

Lamphey Bishop's Palace has been acquired by CADW (Welsh Historic Monuments) who have carried out careful renovation work to give visitors a rich insight into what the building looked like in a bygone age.

Tel: 02920 500200

Top: Penrhos Cottage
Above: Tenby Museum

MILFORD HAVEN MUSEUM

The museum brings to life the fascinating story of the historic waterway and the new town's struggle to fulfil its potential. The Milford Haven story is a cycle of hopes dashed and dreams unfulfilled and covers its brief period as a whaling port, which ended when gas replaced whale oil for lighting the streets of London. It also covers the town's attempts to become a great Trans-Atlantic port, which floundered when the Great Western Railway terminus was built at Neyland and not Milford.

Tel: 01646 694496

PENRHOS COTTAGE

This is a typical North Pembrokeshire thatched cottage that has survived almost unchanged since the 19th Century. Built as an overnight cottage in about 1800 and later rebuilt in stone, Penrhos, with its original Welsh oak furniture, provides a unique opportunity to view the cottager's life in the past.

The cottage is open by appointment. For further details contact Scolton Manor Museum.

Tel: 01437 731328

PENTRE IFAN

Pentre Ifan is a Neolithic burial chamber, dating back from around 3000 BC. Administered by CADW (Welsh Historic Monuments) it can be reached via the A48 from Newport, then follow the signs for Pentre Ifan.

Tel: 02920 500200

SCOLTON MANOR

Scolton Manor is a fine example of a Victorian country house. In recent years it period rooms on three floors have been carefully restored. In addition, two exhibition galleries have also been developed in the house. The collections at Scolton Manor include fine and decorative art, social and industrial history, costume, military history not to mention information on the history of Pembrokeshire.

Tel: 01437 731328

ST. DAVIDS BISHOP'S PALACE

Standing in the shadow of St. Davids Cathedral are the remains of the Bishop's Palace that was destroyed during the 16th Century. However, much still remains to enable visitors to appreciate the scale of the imposing building.

Tel: 01437 720517

TENBY'S MEDIEVAL WALLED TOWN

Tenby's Medieval Walled Town is just one of the many attractions to see during a visit to this popular tourist haven. For more information contact Tenby Museum and Art Gallery.

Tel: 01834 842809

TENBY MUSEUM & ART GALLERY

Established in 1878, this national award-winning museum set in the ruins of a medieval castle is situated on a spectacular site overlooking Carmarthen Bay. Exhibitions of local archaeology, geology, maritime history, natural history and a social history exhibition - "The Story of Tenby". Events programme includes talks, workshops and lectures for children and adults. Museum shop with books, cards, souvenirs and giftware.

The Museum and Art Gallery is open throughout the year. Full access for disabled visitors. Admission charges and concessions apply.

For opening times and more information Tel: 01834 842809

*St. Davids
Bishop's Palace*

"The best £2 I have ever spent, wonderful."

"Worth having a rainy day for!"

"I would recommend it to anybody!"

County Museum, Manor House, Tea Room, Eco-Centre, and Shop set in 60 acres of Park and Woodland

OPENING TIMES
Eco-Centre & Country Park:
Every day except Christmas Day & Boxing Day
April – Oct
9am – 6pm
November – March
9am – 4.30pm

Museum:
Tuesday – Sunday & Bank Holidays,
April – October.
Open Mondays during July & August
10.30am – 1pm,
1.30pm – 5.30pm

HOW TO FIND US

5 miles north of Haverfordwest on the B4329 Cardigan Road

Colby Woodland Gardens (photo courtesy National Trust)

PEMBROKESHIRE'S GARDENS

Pembrokeshire's stunning landscape provides the perfect backdrop to the county's many and varied gardens open to visitors. The following is a brief guide to those well worth a visit.

Barn Court
Templeton, Nr. Narberth
Tel: 01834 861224
Visitors are welcome to wander around the gardens free of charge. Antiques, tea rooms, plants for sale.

Begelly Park Water Garden
Kilgetty, Nr. Tenby
Tel: 01834 811320
Set in 12 acres of natural and landscaped features. Tearooms and lakeside picnic area.

Bro Meigan Gardens
Boncath
Tel: 01239 841232
Inspirational gardens with huge range of planting. Tea room.

Colby Woodland Gardens
near Amroth
Tel: 01834 811885
Eight acres of woodland garden set in a tranquil and secluded valley. Gift shop, tea rooms, gallery and picnic area. Managed by The National Trust.

Manorowen Walled Gardens
Fishguard
Tel: 01348 872168
Walled garden dating back to 1750. Semi-permanent exhibition of sculpture. Picnic area, teas and plants for sale.

Moorland Cottage Plants
Rhyd y Groes, Brynberian, Crymych
Tel: 01239 891363
Small country garden with themed areas, open for charity and with panoramic views of the Preseli mountains.

Newbridge Nursery
Crundale, Nr. Haverfordwest
Tel: 01437 731678
A small, family run nursery where visitors are welcome to enjoy the adjacent gardens including a wildlife meadow, water and bog garden, and a riverside walk.

Penlan Uchaf Gardens
Gwaun Valley, Fishguard
Tel: 01348 881388
Three acres of landscaped gardens set in the beautiful Gwaun Valley.

Picton Castle
Rhos, Haverfordwest
Tel: 01437 751326
40 acres of woodland and walled gardens with a unique collection of rhododendrons

and azaleas, mature trees, unusual shrubs, wild flowers, fern walk, fernery, maze, restored dewpond and herb collection. Spring and Autumn plant sales.

See advert on page 78

Penrallt Garden Centre

Moylegrove, Nr. Cardigan
Tel: 01239 881295

Set in a beautiful location overlooking the sea and coast path above Ceibwr Bay, with a large, comprehensive coll-ection of home grown and unusual plants.

See advert on page 118

Patio & Garden

Wiston, Haverfordwest
Tel: 01437 751343

An extensive range of pots, statues and sundials for patio and garden.

Scolton Manor

Haverfordwest
Tel: 01437 731328

Victorian Manor House, Museum and award-winning Visitor Centre set in 60 acres of country park and wood-lands.

See advert on page 193

Picton Castle

this page:
Aberglasney
Gardens

Upton Castle Gardens

Cosheston, Pembroke
Tel: 01646 651782

35 acres of delightful gardens with a variety of attractions and leading to the shores of the Carew river. Restored 13th century chapel. Managed by The Pembrokeshire Coast National Park Authority

If you fancy a trip further afield an ideal day visit would be to the neighbouring county of Carmarthenshire to witness an outstanding and unique garden venture.

Aberglasney Historic House & Gardens

Llangathen, Carmarthenshire
Tel: 01558 668998

Aberglasney is one of the Country's most exciting garden restoration projects. The Gardens have wonderful horticultural qualities and mysterious history. Within the nine acres of garden are six different garden spaces including three walled gardens. At its heart is a unique and fully restored Elizabethan/Jacobean cloister and parapet walk, giving wonderful views over the Gardens which contain many rare and unusual plants giving interest throughout the year.

The Yew Tunnel is of special interest to visitors. Because the branches were bent over to form a tunnel and not planted as a double row, as far as we know it is unique in the British Isles.

The Cloister Garden is now restored. The design has taken into account the extensive archeological survey that was carried out on the site during 1999. This survey

discovered some of the earliest garden features such as retaining walls and flights of steps, which date back to the late 16th century. Various older artefacts were also discovered including a silver Long Cross Penny dating back to Edward I c1282-1289 and a silver half groat dating back to Henry VII c1485-1509. This perhaps indicates that the site was occupied even earlier than first thought.

The parapet walkway, dating from 1600, is the only example that survives in the U.K.

The walls, cloister, gatehouse and the shell of the house are all now in good condition.

The House and Gardens will continually be improved over the years. The result will be a world renowned Garden set in the hauntingly beautiful and unspoiled pastoral landscape of the Tywi Valley.

Visitors will now be able to enjoy, for the first time, all the seasons of the year in the Garden as Aberglasney will now be open every day, (except Christmas Day).

Our very experienced guides are on hand and are well versed in the historical and horticultural aspect of the Gardens.

As well as a wonderful selection of rare and unusual plants, which have been planted in the woodland areas, together with the amazing tree ferns, there are all manner of birds to be seen throughout the Garden. You may well see a Red Kite circling lazily in the skies overhead.

There is a Cafe in the grounds, which serves delectable light lunches and snacks. In the summer, tea can be taken on the terrace overlooking the Pool Garden. There is also a shop and plant sales area.

See our advert on page 223

this page:
Aberglasney
Gardens

DAY TOURS BY CAR IN PEMBROKESHIRE

For those visitors who like to explore by car, these seven day drives will show you much of Pembrokeshire's varied landscape.

The routes suggested cover the south, west, north and central regions of the county, and each tour brings you back to your original starting point.

All are intended as a leisurely drive with plenty of interesting features along the way.

Tour 1

Tenby - Carew - Llawhaden - Narberth - Amroth - Saundersfoot - Tenby

From Tenby take the B4318 to St. Florence where you can take in the magnificent views across the Ritec Valley. After Mano House Leisure Park, turn lef to the pretty village of S Florence, which features Flemish-style chimney.

Leave St. Florence and return to the B4318, turning left for Sageston. At Sageston follow the A477 toward Pembroke for three-quarter of a mile and then turn right on to the A4075 for Carew which has its own castle, Celtic cross and 17th-century bridge Cross the bridge and proceed up the hill, turning left on the minor road to Cresswell Quay where the estuary is frequented by herons and kingfishers. Then it's on to Lawrenny where at the quay there are yachting facilities, pleasant riverside walks and a picnic site.

Landshipping Quay, the next village you arrive at, offers a tranquil setting with riverside views. From here follow the signs for Minwear and then on to Blackpool Mill where there is a restored mill, cafe, and riverside and woodland walks.

Take the A4075 down the hill to the A40 at Canaston Bridge then left towards Haverfordwest and turn right shortly after to Llawhaden where there is a castle and beautiful parish church. Left over the village bridge takes ou to Pont-Shan where turning right on to the B4314 takes you to the market town of Narberth.

Leave Narberth on the B4314 for Princes Gate, go straight on at the crossroads for Ludchurch and follow the road for Longstone, again going straight on at the next crossroad for Colby Lodge, which features National Trust property and gardens.

From Colby Lodge proceed up the hill to the T-junction and turn right for Amroth, an unspoilt coastal village with shops, pubs, restaurants, superb beach at low tide and seafront parking.

From Amroth drive up the hill to the T-junction at Summerhill, turn left and follow the coast road, passing through Wiseman's Bridge and then on to the popular village resort of Saundersfoot where you'll find superb beaches, tunnel walks to Wiseman's Bridge, shops and restaurants.

From Saundersfoot proceed out of the village up the hill to New Hedges and return to Tenby on the A478.

Tour 2

Tenby - Lydstep - Manorbier - Lamphey - Freshwater-East - Stackpole - Pembroke - Carew - Tenby

Leave Tenby on the A4139 signposted Pembroke and as you approach Lydstep village note the pull-in on the left-

hand side of the road giving superb views of Caldey Island and the cliffs towards Giltar Point.

After passing through Lydstep village, turn left at the crossroads to Manorbier (B4585). For a detour to one of the best beaches in Pembrokeshire, follow the signs to Skrinkle Haven where you'll find good parking. Retrace your steps back to the B4585 and turn left to Manorbier village where there is a Norman castle and church, village shops, pub, cafe and beach.

Leave Manorbier on the B4585 signposted Pembroke and rejoin the A4139, which takes you through Jameston and Hodgeston and on to Lamphey where there is a ruined medieval Bishop's Palace.

From Lamphey rejoin the B4584 to Freshwater East where there is a beach, sand dunes and access to the coastal path.

To reach Stackpole Quay, cross the small narrow bridge

Manorbier Castle

199

Angle

by the beach and follow the road through East Trewent for about 2 miles where you will find a small harbour, large car park, and coast path to Barafundle beach. Return to the T-junction and turn left to the village of Stackpole, following the road through National Trust woodland to the B4319. Turn right for Pembroke where there is a magnificent medieval castle and tourist information centre

To return to Tenby, leave Pembroke along Main Street and follow the signpost for St. Clears. At the major junction with the A477, turn right and after about 2 miles turn left (A4075) at the roundabout for Carew, where there is another medieval castle, Celtic cross, tidal mill, walks, pub, cafe and riverside picnic area. Return to the A477 and turn left. Turn right on to the B4318, signposted Tenby at the roundabout.

Tour 3

Pembroke - Bosherston St. Govan's - Stack Rocks Castlemartin - Freshwater West Angle - Pembroke

From Pembroke take the B4319 for Bosherston. After about 3 miles note St. Petrox Church on your right. Continue, turning left at the signpost for Bosherston (church, lily ponds, fishing, superb walks, wildlife, access to Broadhaven beach, pub and café).

Continue through Bosherston, turning left for Broad Haven where there is a large clifftop car park, outstanding views and a superb beach.

Re-trace the road back to Bosherston, turning left in the village for St Govan's Head which has a remarkable chapel in the cliffs and spectacular views over dramatic coastal features such as Huntsman's Leap.

Back through Bosherston to the B4319 turn left for Castlemartin. After you pass Merrion Camp, where two tanks are on display at the entrance, turn left for Stack Rocks. The road passes medieval Flimston Chapel and leads to a large cliff top car park. Stack Rocks (two vertical columns, home to thousands of breeding seabirds in early summer) stand just offshore a few hundred yards to your left. A short distance to your right is a viewing platform for the

TOUR 3

Green Bridge of Wales, a spectacular limestone arch.

Return to the B4319 and turn left for Castlemartin, where an 18th-century circular stone cattle pound is now a traffic roundabout. Fork left for Freshwater West, noted for its long, wide beach backed by rolling sand dunes, with a restored beach hut once used for drying seaweed to make laverbread.

Continue along the coast road, which gives more superb views as it climbs again towards a T-junction. Turn left here (B4320) for Angle, passing the huge Texaco refinery and views across the estuary towards Milford Haven and the busy shipping lanes.

In the old fishing village of Angle, which lies between East Angle Bay and West Angle Bay, interesting sights include the church and the remains of the medieval Tower House. West Angle Bay has a beach, café, parking, together with views of Thorn Island and the Haven; while East Angle Bay is home to a lifeboat station, yacht moorings, outstanding views and walks. Return to Pembroke on the B4320 via Hundleton.

Tour 4

Haverfordwest - Milford Haven - Dale - Marloes - Little Haven - Broad Haven - Nolton Haven - Newgale - Haverfordwest

Leave Haverfordwest on the A4076, passing through

Johnston towards Milford Haven, which offers easy parking at both the Rath and the marina. Attractions here include a museum, adventure playground, choice of eating places, boat trips, and pleasant walks and views along the Haven waterway.

From Milford Haven, follow the road signposted Herbrandston and Dale, eventually joining the B4327 from Haverfordwest about two and a half miles from Dale which is a mecca for watersport enthusiasts.

Then it's on to St. Ann's Head which features a lighthouse, together with outstanding views of the Atlantic and the entrance to the Haven waterway.

Retrace your journey to Dale from where you can take a detour to West Dale Beach

Haverfordwest

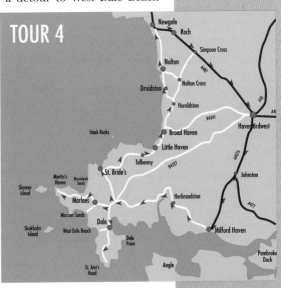

TOUR 4

Newgale
Roch
Simpson Cross
Nolton
A487
Nolton Cross
Druidston
Haroldston
B4341
Haverfordwest
A40
Stack Rocks
Broad Haven
Little Haven
A4076
Talbenny
B4327
Johnston
Martin's Haven
Musselwick Sands
St. Bride's
A477
Skomer Island
Marloes
Herbrandston
Marloes Sands
Dale
Skokholm Island
West Dale Beach
Milford Haven
Dale Point
Pembroke Dock
St. Ann's Head
Angle

by turning left by the church and leaving your car at the end of the road.

After Dale take the B4327 for about one and a half miles and turn left to Marloes where you will discover one of Pembrokeshire's most beautiful beaches at Marloes Sands.

Martins Haven is well worth a visit for here the coast road culminates in a National Trust car park, and a walk from Martin's Haven to the headland will give you outstanding views of Skomer, Skokholm and St. Bride's Bay.

Return to Marloes and follow the signs for Dale, turning left at the T-junction. After about a quarter of a mile turn left for St. Bride's.

Your next port of call is the small, pretty seaside village of Little Haven, which i accessible via various countr lanes that take you throug Talbenny.

From Little Haven follo the road out to Broad Haven where there is easy parking and a haven for water-spor enthusiasts featuring a long beach, outstanding views and walks, interesting rock formations, shops and other facilities.

From Broad Haven take the coast road north for Nolton Haven, which takes you on to Newgale another long beach offering watersports, and views towards nearby St. Davids. From Newgale take the A487 to Haverfordwest, returning via Roch and Simpson Cross.

Marloes Sands

Tour 5

Haverfordwest - Clarbeston Road - Llysyfran - Maenclochog - Rosebush - Gwaun Valley - Dinas Cross - Fishguard - Strumble Head - Mathry - Letterston - Treffgarne Gorge - Haverfordwest

Leave Haverfordwest on the Withybush and Crundale road (B4329) turning right on to the minor road signposted Clarbeston Road and Llysyfran.

Carefully follow the signs for Llysyfran Country Park, where there is a reservoir used for fishing and a visitors centre and restaurant.

From the country park rejoin the road to nearby Gwastad where a short detour to New Moat is well worthwhile. Return to the Gwastad road and go on to the pretty village of Maenclochog. Follow the B4313 to Rosebush, a village whose claim to fame, is that the slates from its quarries were used to roof The Houses of Parliament and continue to the crossroads at New Inn. Here you turn right and climb to one of the highest points of the Preseli Hills, which offers superb views. Return to the crossroads at New Inn, turning right on to the B4313 for Fishguard.

Continue along the B4313 for about 5 miles and turn left down the hill for Pontfaen. After the village bridge go straight on at the crossroads

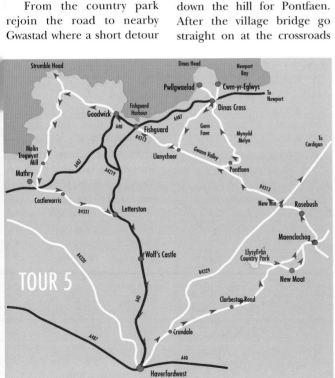

Treffgarne Gorge

and up the very steep hill for Dinas Cross. This moorland road gives outstanding views across Newport Bay before descending to Dinas Cross. At the T-junction turn right on to the A487 and turn immediately left for Pwll-gwaelod.

Return to the A487, turn left and then go left again for Cwm-yr-Eglwys, a picturesque beach featuring a ruined church.

Retrace your steps back to the main road where you turn right for Fishguard. Follow the road for about two miles then turn left to Llanychaer. This road is very narrow and steep in places. After passing over the bridge in the village, rejoin the B4313, turning right for Fishguard, home of the Rosslare to Fishguard Ferry Terminal, passing through picturesque Lower Fishguard, a popular film location.

At the roundabout by the Stena Line terminal, proceed up the hill and follow the sign for Strumble Head where there is a lighthouse and spectacular views of the coastline.

Retracing your steps follow the coast road towards Mathry which features an unusual parish church, stunning views and an ancient burial site nearby.

From there follow the signs for Letterston where you turn right at the crossroads in the village on to the A40 and head back to Haverfordwest via Treffgarne Gorge which offers striking rock formations and spectacular views.

Tour 6

Haverfordwest - Newgale - Solva - Middle Mill - St.Davids - Abereiddy - Porthgain - Abercastle - Trefin - Haverfordwest

Take the A487 out of Haverfordwest signposted St. Davids, passing through Simpson Cross and Roch on to Newgale which offers superb views over St. Bride's Bay.

Next stop is Solva where there is a beautiful natural harbour, pretty village, shops, and excellent walks.

Continuing on this road brings you to the tiny city of St. Davids, which boasts a cathedral, Bishop's Palace, shops, restaurants, art galleries, and outdoor activities, together with an information centre.

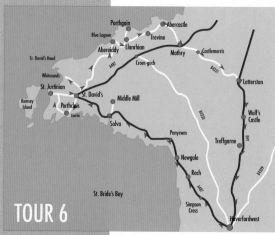

TOUR 6

From St. Davids you can take the minor road to Porth Clais, another picturesque little harbour, and St. Justinian, where there is a RNLI lifeboat station and views across Ramsey Sound.

Returning to St. Davids, follow the signs to Fishguard for a short distance before turning left for Whitesands Bay (or as it's known locally, Traeth Mawr). Here you will find one of the finest beaches in Britain (European Blue Flag Award) and many water sport activities. Return towards the A487 follow the signs for Abereiddy where adjacent to the pebble beach is the Blue Lagoon.

From Abereiddy, follow the coast road to Llanrhian and turn left for Porthgain, which has a history of exporting slate across the world.

Returning to Llanrhian, turn left at the cross roads for Trefin where there is a youth hostel, partly restored mill, hand weaving centre and craft shop. The next harbour along this rugged coastline is Abercastle, home to the Carreg Sampson burial chamber.

Follow the road out of Abercastle for the village of Mathry which brings you back to the B4331 to Letterston, where you turn right on to the A40 and on to Haverfordwest via Treffgarne Gorge and the Nant-y-Coy Mill.

Tour 7

Fishguard - Dinas Cross - Newport - Nevern - Moylegrove - Poppit Sands - St Dogmael's - Cardigan - Gwbert - Mwnt - Llechryd - Cilgerran - Blaenffos - Preseli Hills - Rosebush - Gwaun Valley - Fishguard

Leave Fishguard on the A487 towards Cardigan.

Continue to Newport and Nevern where there is a Celtic Cross and Pilgrims Cross. En route two detours are recommended. The first is to one of Britain's best prehistoric burial chambers - Pentre Ifan, which can be found by turning right off the A487 before the Nevern turn-off and following the narrow country lanes to the top of the hill.

The second detour is to Castell Henllys, a reconstructed Iron Age fort managed by the National Park Authority.

After Nevern proceed on the B4582 and take the third left-hand turn, signposted Moylegrove, an attractive coastal village dating back to Norman times. In the village turn left along the narrow road to the pebble beach at Ceibwr Bay.

From Moylegrove follow the narrow country lanes to Poppit Sands, a large sand beach with car park and lifeboat station, together with views of the Teifi estuary.

Close to Poppit Sands is St Dogmael's, an attractive hillside village that features the ruins of a 12th-century Benedictine abbey and parish church containing the Sagranus Stone.

From St. Dogmael's the road takes you over the bridge to the historic market town of Cardigan and along the northern bank of the River Teifi to Gwbert and then Mwnt. Returning to Cardigan take the A484 to Llechryd and Cilgerran, home to coracles on the Teifi and the Welsh Wildlife Centre.

From Cilgerran drive to Rhos-Hill where you join the A478 and the village of Crymych. On leaving the village, go through Mynachlogddu along a country road that takes you through the heart of the Preseli Hills.

Return towards the village and follow the signpost for Rosebush.

Continue to the crossroads at New Inn and go straight on for Fishguard where the road takes you alongside the beautiful Gwaun Valley, and offers detours to the villages of Pontfaen and Llanychaer.

Newport

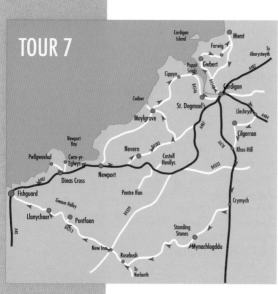

TOUR 7

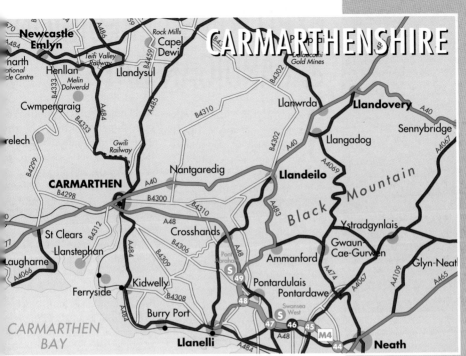

Newcastle Emlyn
A484
A486
A486
narth
ational
cle Centre
Rock Mills
Capel Dewi
A475
Teifi Valley Railway
A459
Henllan
Melin Dolwerdd
A484
Llandysul
Cwmpengraig
A4333
relech
B4299
Gwili Railway
A483
Nantgaredig
CARMARTHEN
B4298
A40
B4300
B4310
Dolaucothi Gold Mines
A482
Llanwrda
A4302
Llandovery
A40
Sennybridge
A4067
Llangadog
A40
A4069
Llandeilo
A483
Black Mountain
A483
A48
Crosshands
B4306
B4309
A48
A484
B4312
B4310
Ystradgynlais
Gwaun-Cae-Gurwen
A474
A4067
Glyn-Neath
A109
A4109
A465
St Clears
Llanstephan
Pont Sarah?
S 49
Ammanford
A474
A4067
Llandeilo
77
Laugharne
A4066
Kidwelly
B4308
Ferryside
A484
Burry Port
Pontardulais
Pontardawe
48
Swansea West
47 46 45
A48
M4
44
Neath
CARMARTHEN BAY
Llanelli
A484

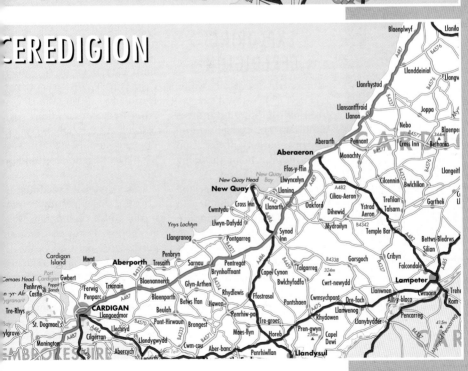

Blaenplwyf
Llanila
A487
B4576
Llanddeiniol
B4337
Llangw
Llanrhystud
A576
Llansantffraid Llanon
B4337
Joppa
CAR
Nebo
Blaenpl
344m
Aberarth
Pennant
B4577
Cross Inn
Bethania
Aberaeron
Monachty
B4577
Cilcennin
Bwlchllan
A575
Llangeith
Ffos-y-ffin
New Quay Bay
A482
Ciliau-Aeron
Trefilan
Gartheli
C
New Quay Head
Llwyncelyn
Oakford
Dihewid
Ystrad Aeron
Talsarn
NEW QUAY
Llanina
A487
A482
Temple Bar
A485
Bettws-Bledrws
Cross Inn
Llanarth
Mydroilyn
B4342
Silian
Cwmtydu
A4342
Synod Inn
A486
Gorsgoch
Cribyn
Falcondale
Ynys Lochtyn
Llwyn-Dafydd
Pontgarreg
B4337
Llampeter
A485
Langranog
Penbryn
Pentregat
B4338
Cwrt-newydd
Llanwnen
Cwmann
Trehe
Cardigan Island
Mwnt
Aberporth
Tresaith
Sarnau
Brynhoffnant
Talgarreg
324m
Dre-fach
Allt-y-blaca
Ram
Cemaes Head
Port Cardigan
Gwbert
Ferwig
Tremain
Blaenannerch
Glyn-Arthen
Capel Cynon
Bwlchyfadfa
Cwmsychpant
A475
Pencarreg
415m
Penbryn-yr-Afr
Poppit Sands
Penparc
Blaenporth
Betws Ifan
Rhydlewis
Ffostrasol
Pontshaen
Rhydowen
Llanwenog
Llanybydder
B457
Tre-Rhys
CARDIGAN
Llangoedmor
Hawen
Penrhiw-pal
Llanwnnen
Bay
St. Dogmael's
Beulah
Pont-Hirwaun
Brongest
Tre-groes
Pren-gwyn
256m
Capel Dewi
ylgrove
Monington
A487
Llechryd
Cilgerran
Llandygwydd
B4570
Maes-llyn
Horeb
CAR
EMBROKESHIRE
Abercych
Aber-banc
Penrhiwllan
LLANDYSUL

Newquay

EXPLORING CEREDIGION & CARDIGAN BAY

Just across the Teifi estuary from Poppit Sands and St. Dogmaels is the ancient county of Cardiganshire, or Ceredigion as it is now known in Welsh.

Like Pembrokeshire it is a county with a rich and varied landscape together with a long and dramatic history and is well-known to countless holidaymakers as the home of such popular seaside resorts as New Quay, Aberaeron and Aberystwyth. Its spectacular coastline is marked by many fine beaches.

EXPLORING CEREDIGION

Historic Cardigan, which received its first Royal Charter in 1199 from King John, is an important holiday centre and thriving market town and is one of the main shopping centres for the region.

Beautifully sited near the mouth of the River Teifi with some of Wales' most attractive coast and countryside right on the doorstep, its shops and narrow streets retain the town's character. The Market Hall, built in 1859 and featuring impressive stone arches, holds a general market twice weekly and a livestock market once a week.

Visitor attractions include the Theatr Mwldan (housed in the same building as the Tourist Information Centre both of which are open all year round), an indoor leisure centre, a golf club at nearby Gwbert, and a large annual arts festival, Gwyl Fawr Aberteifi.

Crossing the Teifi below the castle is the striking multi-arched stone bridge. Sources disagree as to whether this is the original Norman Bridge, strengthened and widened in later years, or whether it was constructed in the 17th or even 18th century. The history of Cardigan Castle raises less argument. The ruins that now remain date from 1240, and it must have been in an earlier castle that the very first National Eisteddfod - advertised, for a whole year beforehand throughout Wales, England and Scotland - was hosted by Rhys ap Gruffudd in 1176.

The National Eisteddfod is now the major cultural event in the Welsh calendar, as well as being Europe's largest peripatetic cultural festival. Cardigan Castle, like so many others, was destroyed by Cromwell, and now all that remains is privately owned.

More recently, Cardigan was one of Wales' most prominent ports having as many as 300 ships registered

Aberaeron

here. Shipbuilding thrived in the 19th century when the busy warehouses along the waterfront handled everything from exports of herring, corn, butter and slate to imports of limestone, salt, coal, timber for shipbuilding, and manufactured goods. Human cargo was carried too: emigrant ships sailed from Cardigan to New York in the USA and New Brunswick in Canada.

This prosperous period for Cardigan was relatively short-lived. Inevitably, booming trade meant that ships were getting bigger all the time while the gradual silting of the estuary was making access to Cardigan more and more restricted. The final nail in the town's coffin as a commercial port was the coming of the railway in 1885 - but today, as a popular holiday destination, Cardigan is once again a busy centre of attention, boasting many attractions within easy reach. Several of these stand near the banks of the Teifi, such as St. Dogmael's Abbey, Poppit Sands, the Welsh Wildlife Centre, Cilgerran Castle and Cenarth Falls.

Theatr Mwldan

A vibrant theatre and cinema with a varied programme of all the latest cinema releases and cultural films plus a fantastic top-quality line-up of music, drama and dance. Theatr Mwldan is one of Wales' leading arts and entertainment centres and an essential stop for anyone!

For programme details and bookings, ring the box office on 01239 621200, or see www.mwldan.co.uk

Cardigan Swimming Pool & Leisure Complex

Situated in the heart of Cardigan Town at the Main Fairfield Car Park, the Centre has 2 pools, one a 25 metre pool which is available for adult, public and fun sessions, and the other a toddler therapy pool which is regularly

hired for parties and clubs. The very popular 'Challenge' inflatable can be hired on request.

The dry side, for those who prefer terra firma, boasts a superb fitness suite called Lifestyle where you can exercise all major parts of the body with user friendly weight stacks, plus an excellent range of Lifefitness Cardio Vascular machines of which there are Lifecycles, Treadmills and Steppers Cross Trainer Recumbent Cycle. You can pay by the session, monthly or quarterly. The latter two will get you free swims and saunas.

An induction and programm facility is available, for which small charge is payable bu usually compensated by fre sessions.

Other facilities within th complex include an Ergolin contoured fast tannin sunbed, sports hall for mult ple use, and sauna (booking i advisable). There is a loung area and viewing galler upstairs with no charge fo spectators.

For more information rin 01239 613632 or email:manage @swimming35.freeserve.co.uk

Cilgerran Castle

Cilgerran Castle, three miles southeast of Cardigan, is perched in a dramatic position on a high bluff above the River Teifi. Seen from the deep wooded gorge below - as it was for centuries by the coracle fishermen - it presents a spectacular sight, which inspired great landscape artists such as Turner and Richard Wilson. Equally, the views, which visitors can enjoy from its ruined towers, are magnificent.

The castle, small by comparison with Pembroke and the great Norman fortresses of North Wales, is mainly 13th century, but despite its apparently unassailable position, it changed hands many times between the 12th and 14th centuries. Taken from the Normans by Lord Rhys in 1164, it was recaptured in 1204 by William Marshall; used as a base by Llewellyn the Great in 1215, when he summoned a Council of all Wales at Aberystwyth; taken again by the Normans in 1223, following which the present towers were built. After a period of decline and then refortification in the 14th century, the castle was captured again for a brief period by the Welsh in 1405 during the uprising of Owain Glyndwr.

Felinwynt Rainforest Centre

Visit this mini-rainforest and experience a different world. Wander amongst exotic plants and tropical butterflies accompanied by the sounds of the Peruvian Amazon. Waterfalls and streams enhance the humidity and someone is on hand most of the time to explain the mysteries of butterflies and to answer any questions.

The visitor centre comprises of the nature gift shop and an excellent cafe, serving meals and snacks all day (why not try one of Dorothy's homemade cakes!)

View towards Cardigan Island

Talyllyn Railway

The centre is suitable for the disabled. Crayons and paper are provided free for children to create pictures for display in the gallery.

The Centre can be found 6 miles from Cardigan and 4 miles from Aberporth; follow the brown signs from the A487 at Blanannerch.

For more information ring 01239 810250 or 810882.

Talyllyn Railway
Wharf Station, Tywyn

The main station of the narrow gauge Talyllyn Railway is at Tywyn on the mid-Wales coast. From there, the line runs inland for over seven miles to Nant Gwernol, most of the route being in Snowdonia National Park. Built in 1865 to bring slate to the coast, the Railway was taken over by the Talyllyn Railway Preservation Society in 1951, becoming the first preserved railway in the world.

The railway operates daily from the end of March to the first week in November, and at Christmas. All passenger trains are hauled by coal fired steam locomotives.

Tywyn Wharf station has a shop and new enlarged café. Also new is The Narrow Gauge Railway Museum with exhibits from over 70 railways. A special section is devoted to

Rev. W Audrey and his 'Railway Series' of children's books, many of which were inspired by the Talyllyn where Rev. Audrey worked as a volunteer guard. Abergynolwyn has a café and shop and the popular Railway Adventure children's playground. At Dolgoch there are spectacular waterfalls with a tea room at the nearby Dolgoch Falls Hotel. A booklet detailing walks from every station on the line is available, and as every round trip ticket is a Day Rover, there are lots of opportunities to explore this beautiful part of Wales.

For details of timetable and special events tel: 01654 710472 www.talyllyn.co.uk

Welsh Wildlife Centre, Cilgerran

This rare wildlife experience is located just south of Cardigan and offers visitors the opportunity to enjoy the wonders of the diverse wildlife of west Wales.

The Centre, comprising of meadows, woodland, reed beds, marsh and riverside, is the home to some of Britain's most picturesque and exciting wildlife.

It houses some of the most endangered habitats where rare and fragile species are coming back from the brink of extinction. Breeds like the Red Kite, Cetti's Warbler, Marsh Harrier and the Little Egret are just some of the regular visitors to this unique nature reserve.

The Centre is also home to otters and a wonderful display of rare wild flowers.

Other countryside wildlife like deer, badgers, shrews, voles and bats can also be seen on the reserve, which offers seven different habitats.

The Welsh Wildlife Centre offers weather-proof hides with seating for bird watching at one of the UK's top ornithological sites. The Visitor Centre includes a wildlife display, has facilities for the disabled and offers educational facilities for schools. It also includes a restaurant and gift shop. A full programme of events and activities for all ages runs throughout the season.

For further information ring: 01239 621600, e-mail: wildlife@wtww.co.uk or visit their website at www.wtsww.co.uk

Talyllyn Railway

The Wicker Otter

Carmarthen

EXPLORING CARMARTHENSHIRE

armarthenshire is a very attractive holiday destination for visitors who appreciate history, culture and a green and beautiful environment. Covering an area of 1,000 square miles, the county is a veritable feast of delights and discovery - an intoxicating mix of glorious coast and countryside, offering a wealth of activities.

The 50 miles of stunning coastline embrace vast stretches of safe golden sands, such as the beaches of Cefn Sidan and Pendine, punctuated by the Taf and Towy estuaries, which so inspired the legendary writer Dylan Thomas. The Loughor estuary, a favourite haunt of migratory birds, is famous for its cockles - a delicacy to be found in the markets of Llanelli and Carmarthen.

The unspoilt and contrasting countryside of Carmarthenshire touches the edge of the Brecon Beacons National Park in the east, the Cambrian Mountains in the north and the picturesque Teifi Valley to the west.

The county is also rich in bustling market towns, such as Newcastle Emlyn, Llandysul, Whitland, Llandeilo, Llandovery, and Llanybydder and of course Carmarthen.

The attractions and activities to be enjoyed in Carmarthenshire are many and varied - from castles museums and art galleries steam railways, country parks, fishing and golf to the beautiful gardens a Aberglasney; not forgetting of course, all that warm Welsh hospitality.

CARMARTHEN

At the heart of the county is the ancient township of Carmarthen, the reputed birthplace of Merlin - wizard and counsellor to King Arthur. The town stands eight miles inland on the River Towy - a position that inspired the Romans to make it their strategic regional capital. They also built an amphitheatre here, rediscovered in 1936 but not excavated until 1968.

Today, Carmarthen's quaint old narrow streets are full of Welsh character and tradition. There's also a first-class modern shopping centre with its many familiar high street names, which expanded with the opening of the Greyfriars shopping complex. Carmarthen's famous market, which is open six days a week, complements the town centre and attracts people from all over Wales.

In Carmarthen you're also likely to catch more than a smattering of Welsh, as it is still widely spoken here. It is believed that the oldest manuscript in the Welsh language - The Black Book of Carmarthen - now in the National Library of Wales in Aberystwyth - was written in the town.

For sport, there's the town's modern leisure centre, with its outstanding all-weather facilities. A few miles west is Derllys Court Golf Club, near Bancyfelin, which has an interesting 9-hole, pay as you play, par 35 course, set in a beautiful location amongst rolling countryside. Another 9 holes were opened in summer 2004. There is a licensed bar together with catering facilities and a warm welcome is extended to visitors. For more information ring 01267 211575.

Another attraction virtually on Carmarthen's doorstep is the Gwili Railway at Bronwydd Arms (just off the A484) - one of Wales' last remaining standard-gauge steam railways where a train takes you to a wooded riverside area deep in the valley where there is also a picnic site. The railway opened in 1860 and eventually became the property of British Railways, but after the remaining milk traffic was

Llansteffan Castle
© Wales Tourist Board

*Dylan Thomas'
Boathouse at
Laugharne*

transferred to road, the line closed in 1973.

The Gwili Railway Company was set up in 1975 and in 1978, and thanks to volunteers a section of the line just over a mile long was reopened between the Bronwydd Arms and the riverside station at Llwyfan Cerrig. An extension towards Cynwyl Elfed is progressing well.

CARMARTHEN BAY

South of Carmarthen, the River Towy emerges into Carmarthen Bay alongside the rivers Taf and Gwendraeth. This is an area of outstanding natural beauty, where scores of waders and seabirds take rich pickings from the broad expanse of mudflats formed by the three estuaries.

Here too you will discover the charming seaside villages of Ferryside and Llansteffan, at the mouth of the Towy. Just a short hop west to the Taf estuary takes you to Laugharne.

LAUGHARNE

An ancient and interesting township standing on the west bank of the Tâf estuary. Originally a fortified Roman station, the township is thought to have been founded

by the Princes of Dynevor prior to the Norman conquest. It has enjoyed several names over the centuries, Abercorran (at the mouth of the Corran), Tallachar, Thalacharne and modern day Laugharne. The town is dominated by the castle which was built in Norman times as part of a line of fortified garrisons along the Carmarthenshire and Pembrokeshire coast designed to keep the local inhabitants under control. It has had a varied history and played a prominent role in the Civil War when it withstood a Cromwellian siege for seven days. More recently, CADW spent twenty years carrying out sympathetic restoration work and it is now open to the public. Laugharne and Malmesbury in Wiltshire are the only towns in the UK to retain their ancient Charter, granted not by Parliament, but by Royal decree and which allows them to be governed by a Corporation in addition to the normal local government bodies. The Corporation is headed by the Portreeve with a Foreman, a Recorder, two Common Attorneys, four Constables, a Baliff and a Jury consisting of twenty Burgesses. This august body of men meets on a monthly basis and many matters of local interest are discussed and decided upon. These sittings are held in the Town Hall where the original Charter is displayed together with many other articles of historic interest. Once every three years, the local population of Laugharne take part in the Common Walk when the boundaries of the Township are walked and identified. This is a walk of some twenty six miles through very rough and difficult countryside and for those brave enough to take part, refreshments are served during the route.

In more recent times Laugharne became the home of the famous Welsh poet, Dylan Thomas and his well known work - Under Milk Wood - was undoubtedly inspired by the Township and its inhabitants. His home, The Boathouse, is now a museum to his life and works and is open to the public.

From Laugharne, the road west cuts a picturesque route to Pendine Sands, where Sir Malcolm Campbell and others made several attempts on the world landspeed record, the most recent being in 1998. The fatal crash of Parry Thomas-Jones in 1927 ended Pendine's racing career, but the exciting new Museum of Speed recalls this village resort's days of fame and glory.

On the eastern side of Carmarthen Bay are the estuaries of the Gwendraeth and Loughor, and the superb seven-mile beach of Cefn Sidan Sands - one of the best beaches in Britain.

CARMARTHEN
MYRTLE HILL, PENSARN

TELEPHONE: **01267 220861**

OPEN 7.30am - 11pm SEVEN DAYS A WEEK

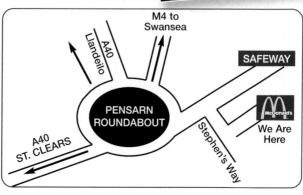

The Stable Door, Laugharne

Whatever your taste in food - one of the finest places to eat in Carmarthenshire is The Stable Door in Laugharne.

Here you will find a choice of menu to suit everyone's pallet - whether it is something spicy or the more traditional fare.

The culinary skills are provided by Wendy Joy, proprietor and chef, who settled in Laugharne in 1998 after years of travelling abroad and various careers that culminated in her providing food for many famous people.

The menu at The Stable Door is as diverse as Wendy's background. It mirrors her travels and experiences and incorporates the best of Thai, Indian, Italian and British dishes. Vegetarians too are catered for and can enjoy some of Wendy's interesting vegetarian dishes.

The Stable Door has a restaurant area, a large conservatory dining area and in good weather you can also eat out in the truly delightful and imaginative garden. There is a beautiful view of Laugharne Castle and the estuary from the dining areas.

For more information ring 01994 427777.

WHITLAND

Whitland, which stands on the River Taf inside the Carmarthenshire border, west of St. Clears, rose in prominence as a market town in the 19th century. The coming of the railway established it as an important junction.

The town's most significant place in history goes back to the 10th century, when the great Welsh king Hywel Dda (Hywel the Good) called an assembly of wise men here to draw up a unified legal code for Wales, based on the ancient tribal laws and customs already in existence. The assembly took place at Ty Gwyn

Laugharne Castle

Llanelli

ar Daf (The White House on the Taf) - Hywel Dda's hunting lodge. It is thought that the house could have been the site chosen two centuries later for Whitland Abbey. The Hywel Dda Interpretive Gardens and Centre, in the centre of the town, now commemorate this great assembly.

Whitland Abbey was the first Cistercian monastery in Wales and gave rise to seven others, including Strata Florida which was founded in 1140, but unfortunately virtually nothing remains of the abbey today, its ruins standing to the north of Whitland.

LLANELLI

Once the tinplate capital of the world, and arguably the home of Welsh rugby, Llanelli is a thriving town with an impressive pedestrianised shopping centre and bustling indoor and outdoor markets.

Standing on the beautiful Loughor estuary, Llanelli has a pleasant beach and is close to many major attractions. These include the recently developed Millennium Coastal Park, Pembrey Country Park, magnificent Cefn Sidan Sands, the Pembrey Motorsports Centre and Kidwelly Castle. Places to visit in Llanelli itself include Parc Howard and Sandy Water Park.

CASTLES

Carmarthenshire boasts several outstanding examples of Norman castles. One of the best-preserved medieval fort-resses in Wales is Kidwelly Castle, while the imposing ruins at Carreg Cennen and Llansteffan both enjoy spectacular elevated positions.

Laugharne Castle, where Dylan Thomas wrote Portrait of the Artist as a Young Dog, has been extensively refurbished by CADW (Welsh Historic Monuments) and is now open to visitors.

Dinefwr Castle, near Llandeilo, is another sight not to be missed.

CENARTH

Cenarth is one of the most popular beauty spots in the whole of West Wales. Standing on the River Teifi, it is a very pretty village, famous for its salmon-leap falls. It is also recognised as the traditional home of the Teifi coracle, and here you will find the National Coracle Centre, which despite its name is a private enterprise, though no less important or interesting for that.

Unspoilt Cenarth is a designated conservation area, with many of its buildings listed. The fine old bridge is believed to be 18th century, and the flourmill, which houses the Coracle Centre, dates from the 1600's. Also of historical interest are St. Llawddog's church and its mysterious Sarsen Stone.

Coracle Centre & Mill, Cenarth

The strange, round fishing boat, known as the coracle, has been a familiar sight on the River Teifi for centuries. It's light, manoeuverable and ideal in shallow water, though mastering the art of coracle fishing can take years of practice. Today there are still 12 pairs licensed to fish on the Teifi, but the best place to see coracles is the National Coracle Centre which houses over 20 different types of coracle, in varying shapes and sizes, from all over the world -

India, Vietnam, Tibet, Iraq and North America - as well as 9 varieties of Welsh coracle and examples from England, Ireland and Scotland. An added bonus for visitors is that in the workshop you can see how coracles are made.

The Centre stands on the ground floor of a 17th-century flourmill, which is also open to visitors, and there are arts, crafts, souvenirs and gifts for sale.

Glyn-Coch Craft Centre, Pwll-Trap, St Clears

The Jones family invite you to our craft centre, set in tranquil countryside, and sign-posted from the A40, - 1 mile west of St Clears. Our Craft Shop sells over 1000 stock lines made by about 30 local suppliers. Some only sell through us. Glyn-Coch Design China was decorated here from 1980 until they moved to Tenby in 1995. We maintain the tradition by Hand Painting China and Glass, and producing our own earthenware

'You can have a go or attend a variety of informal courses'

Cenarth

We also sell wool, woollen garments, and craft kits using wool from our own Rare Norfolk Horn Sheep, which can be seen from our circular Woodland Walk and Nature Trail. After-wards you can relax in our friendly Tearoom, or visit our small displays of Radios, Computers, or Vintage Farm Machinery. Open 7 days a week all year.

For more information ring 01994 231867.

The Bunch of Grapes

The Bunch of Grapes is an attractive Public House built with stone from the castle and oak stolen from Kent! It retains a traditional feel in both its ambience and tasteful decor with a wealth of oak beams. There is a covered interior garden with vines and cacti. The colourful garden at the rear is very sheltered and an excellent suntrap. The pub always has three real ales and Czechoslovakian Budvar, and was CAMRA Pub of the Year for 2004.

For further information phone 01239 711185.

Museum of the Welsh Woollen Industry, Drefach Velindre

Re-opening in spring 2004 following a major redevelopment scheme, the new museum promises not only to do justice to the fascinating story of wool but also continue in commercial production, producing fabrics in traditional patterns and re-interpreting designs for a contemporary market. Imaginative displays, a new cafe and shop selling the very best of Welsh textiles are just some of the treats in store for visitors. The museum has facilities for the disabled and admission is free. Located 4 miles east of Newcastle Emlyn, 16 miles west of Carmarthen. Follow the brown tourist signs for National Woollen Museum.

For more information ring 01559 370929.

Teifi Valley Railway

A short but very enjoyable journey by narrow gauge railway into the beautiful Teifi Valley is the pleasure awaiting you at Henllan Station, between Newcastle Emlyn and Llandysul. A quarter of a mile ride on a Miniature Railway, which although only 20 minutes long is a delightful experience for all ages.

For timetable and other enquiries ring 01559 371077.

Aberglasney, Llangathen, Carmarthenshire

One of the country's most exciting garden restoration projects with wonderful horticultural qualities and a mysterious history. Set within nine acres, there are six different garden spaces including three walled gardens.

Visitors will now be able to enjoy, for the first time, all the seasons of the year in the Garden as Aberglasney will now be open every day, (except Christmas Day).

Our very experienced guides are on hand and are well versed in the historical and horticultural aspect of the Gardens.

As well as a wonderful selection of rare and unusual plants, which have been planted in the woodland areas, together with the amazing tree ferns, there are all manner of birds to be seen throughout the Garden. The House and Gardens will continually be improved over the years. The result will be a world renowned Garden set in the hauntingly beautiful and unspoiled pastoral landscape of the Tywi Valley.

For more information see Gardens Section or ring 01558 668998.

Aberglasney

Aberglasney Historic House & Gardens

Open every day (except Christmas Day) • Summer opening times: 10.00am - 6.00pm (Last entry 5.00pm)
Winter opening times: 10.30am - 4.00pm

Situated between Llandeilo and Carmarthen, 400 yards from the A40 at Broad Oak.

Llangathen, Carmarthenshire, SA32 8QH

Tel/Fax:(01558) 668998

E-Mail: info@aberglasney.org.uk   www.aberglasney.org

Excellent Shop, Plant Sales & Café Facilities

WHERE to eat out

CEREDIGION

CARDIGAN

Caffi'r Castell

Licensed restaurant and cafe serving wholesome home cooked food from traditional Welsh recipes   *see page no. 210*

FELINWYNT

Felinwynt Rainforest & Butterfly Centre

Excellent cafe, serving meals and snacks all day, and mouthwatering homemade cakes   *see page no. 211*

CARMARTHENSHIRE

McDonalds Restaurant

Good fast food for the whole family   *see page no. 218*

LAUGHARNE

The Stable Door Restaurant

Imaginative home cooked meals with varied wine list in a conservatory dining area overlooking the castle and estuary   *see page no. 219*

NEWCASTLE EMLYN

The Bunch of Grapes

Genuine homemade dishes and vegetarian specialities served in the bar or restaurant   *see page no. 222*

PWLL-TRAP

Glyn Coch Studios

Small tea room offering a variety of light snacks and cream teas which are also served in sheltered garden   *see page no. 221*

If you wish to be included in our next "Where to eat" section of this guide then please telephone us on 01646 682296 for further details.

Pembrokeshire Produce Mark

ant to make sure you're getting the
·ery best Pembrokeshire produce?

`hether you're eating out or shop-
ping locally, look out for the
Pembrokeshire Produce Mark.

The Produce Mark is an instantly
·cognisable logo, which shows that
the product you are buying has
been made in Pembrokeshire.

·If displayed in a hospitality establishment, it shows that local pro-
·ace is used within the menu. Retail
utlets displaying the Produce Mark
·ll local products within their shop.

There are currently well over 200
members of the Pembrokeshire
Produce Mark scheme. Before
being able to display the logo, all
·embers of the scheme are verified
to ensure eligibility.

www.pembrokeshire.gov.uk

Haverfordwest Farmers' Market

·uy and taste local Pembrokeshire
produce at the Farmers' Market
on the Riverside Quay,
Haverfordwest 9.00am - 3.00pm

Dates for 2005

January 7th & 21st
February 4th & 18th
March 4th & 18th
April 1st, 15th & 29th
May 13th & 27th
June 10th & 24th
July 8th & 22nd
August 5th & 19th
September 2nd, 16th & 30th
October 14th & 28th
November 11th & 25th
December 9th & 23rd

PEMBROKESHIRE FISH WEEK

HAVE A WHALE OF A TIME IN PEMBROKESHIRE FISH WEEK!

One of Britain's most spectacular stretches of coastline is gearing up for its annual festival of everything fresh and fishy.

Pembrokeshire Fish Week celebrates the abundance of the county's delicious fish and seafood.

The 2005 festival is packed full of family-friendly activities, including cookery demonstrations, fishing competitions, island boat trips, and much more.

Food-lovers can enjoy paella evenings, sushi tastings and chowder nights, and lots of opportunities to sample fresh local produce at fish and shellfish cookery demonstrations by celebrity chefs.

If you'd like to explore the stunning Pembrokeshire coastline, there's lots to choose from - including coastal and island rambles, sea angling trips, nature watches, family seashore safaris, and evening boat trips.

There's also plenty on offer for keen and amateur anglers, from Learn to Fish days to open sea angling and fishing competitions.

Pembrokeshire Fish Week is truly a county-wide event with well over 120 hospitality establishments taking part. Get hooked and have yourself a lot of fun!

Pembrokeshire Fish Week 2005 takes place between June 25th and July 3rd and is organised by Pembrokeshire County Council.

For more information, pick up a festival brochure of events in one of the county's Tourist Information Centres or contact the Council's Food Officer Kate Morgan on 01437 776168 or email kate.morgan@pembrokeshire.gov.uk

Stena Line

With a choice of fast and superferry crossings, unrivalled service and value fares, Stena Line's Fishguard - Rosslare route is the best choice for travel to the south-east and south-west of Ireland.

For people in a hurry, the Stena Lynx III catamaran travels across the sea in a time of just 1 hour 50 minutes.

This Express service makes up to three return crossings daily during the peak period. Alternatively, the luxury super-ferry is ideal for motorists wanting a rest and relaxing break, especially those with children.

There are a number of facilities on board both vessels, including bars, restaurants, Stena Shopping and our exclusive Stena Plus Lounge where you can travel in style and relax in comfort.

From spring to autumn, holidaymakers in Pembrokeshire can take advantage of the hi-speed service and spend a day in the sunny South East of Ireland.

For longer stays, Stena Line Holidays offers a great choice of short breaks in hotels and self catering holidays for all the family, throughout Ireland.

SOUTH EAST IRELAND

A medieval fortress that has stood witness to many key moments in Irish history, a beautifully restored castle that has stood guard over a city for over 900 years...

History you can touch and feel is all around in the South East region, an area linked by a network of five ancient river valleys and containing Ireland's oldest city, Waterford.

Follow the trail of previous visitors, Celts, Vikings and Normans through magnificent castles and ancient monuments, heritage museums and great country houses.

Discover the creative heart of Ireland's traditional crafts and some of Europe's most beautiful gardens, cruise on Ireland's second largest river or enjoy game, sea and coarse angling in the cleaning of rivers and lakes or off miles of stunning coastline.

A Perfect Day

Explore 10,000 years of Irish history in a day! Begin with the Irish National Heritage Park in Wexford and discover how the Irish lived from the Stone Age to the 12th century.

Travel to Waterford and its fabulous Museum of Treasures, tracing the history of Ireland's most ancient city, before lunch in a centuries old pub.

See how the world famous Waterford Crystal is made, then journey to the marvellous castles of Lismore and Cahir and then the magical Rock of Cashel before ending your day at Kilkenny Castle, dining at one of medieval Kilkenny's superb restaurants.

Above: Kilkenny Castle

Below:
The Rock of Cashel

Irish Ferries

Irish Ferries operate to Rosslare on the south east coast of Ireland with the luxury 34,000 ton cruise ferry the m.v. Isle of Inishmore.

You have the choice of afternoon or early morning sailings, and the crossing takes just under 4 hours. The crossing takes you down the Milford Haven Waterway and out past the 2 bird sanctuary Islands of Skokholm and Skomer before heading across St.Georges Channel to the Tusker Rock Light House which is seen approximately half an hour before arriving in Rosslare Harbour. The vessel has 2 Restaurants, Bars and Lounges, plus a childrens free cinema, and a 'Cyber Zone' with electronic games and entertainment. During the summer period there is a live entertainment programme onboard, also a Tourist Information Centre giving information on South Wales and South East Ireland.

Throughout the year we offer low cost Day Trips for visitors to the area, and early spring or autumn money saving offers for passengers with cars. Irish Ferries Holidays also have a great choice of inclusive short and long break holidays in hotels, self catering and motoring holidays for all the family throughout Ireland.

WHAT'S ON IN PEMBROKESHIRE 2005

Date	Event	Phone
March 27 & 28	Oakwood's Live Barney Show	01834 891376
May 6 - 10	Haverfordwest May Fair	01437 763427
May 28 - June 5	St David's Cathedral Festival	
June 24 - July 3	Pembroke Dock Festival	01646 684410
June 25 - July 3	Pembrokeshire Fish Week	01437 776168
June 25	Narberth Castle Grand Opening	01834 860788
July 2 - 10	Llangwm Festival	01437 890841
July 23 - 30	Fishguard International Music Festival	01348 873612
July 29 - August 30	Oakwood's After Dark	01834 891376
July 24 - 30	Narberth Civic Week & Carnival	01834 860788
July 31	Tenby Summer Spectacular	
August 5	La Traviata by Verdi, Lampeter House	01834 869380
August 14	Tenby Summer Spectacular	
August 16 - 18	Pembrokeshire County Show (Agricultural)	
August 30	Frenni Food Festival Crymych	01239 831455
September 23 - 25	Narberth Food Festival	01834 860268
September 17 - 24	Tenby Arts Festival	
October 26 - 30	Oakwood's Eerie Evenings	01834 891376
November	Narbeth Winter Festival & Carnival	01834 860788
December 3	Tenby Winter Carnival	01834 842345
December 10	Pembroke Dock Winter Carnival	01646 684410

Please check out a current Pembrokeshire Event List at:
www.eventsinpembrokeshire.com

The above are only a selection of the many and varied events throughout Pembrokeshire. For more information call in to any Tourist Information Centre, and check out the local press.

Ceredigion Craft Makers 2005

Thursday 24th March 2005 to Tuesday 29th March 2005
at The Band Stand, Aberystwyth.

Friday 24th June 2005 to Sunday 26th June 2005
on The Square Field, Aberaeron.

Wednesday 7th September 2005 to Saturday
10th September 2005 at The Band Stand Aberystwyth.

Secretary: Karen Cocksedge - Tel: 01974 272026

www.ccmcrafts.co.uk

INDEX